Human Origins

Human Origins

EDITED BY

JOHN R. DURANT

Staff Tutor in Biological Sciences,
Department for External Studies,
University of Oxford.

CLARENDON PRESS · OXFORD
1989

Oxford University Press, Walton Street, Oxford OX2 6DP

Oxford New York Toronto
Delhi Bombay Calcutta Madras Karachi
Petaling Jaya Singapore Hong Kong Tokyo
Nairobi Dar es Salaam Cape Town
Melbourne Auckland
and associated companies in
Berlin Ibadan

Oxford is a trade mark of Oxford University Press

Published in the United States
by Oxford University Press, New York

British Library Cataloguing in Publication Data
Human origins.
1. Man. Evolution
I. Durant, John R.
573.2
ISBN 0–19–857612–9

Library of Congress Cataloging in Publication Data
Human origins/edited by John R. Durant.
p. cm.
Includes index.
1. Human evolution. I. Durant, John R.
GN281.H848 1988 573.2—dc19 88–12037
ISBN 0–19–857612–9

Set by Colset Private Limited, Singapore.
Printed in Great Britain by
Butler & Tanner Ltd, Frome, Somerset

Preface

Modern science deals with only a very few questions that are truly fundamental. Three of the most outstanding are: what is the nature and origin of the universe? what is the nature and origin of life? and what is the nature and origin of humankind? The first of these questions constitutes the subject matter of cosmology, while the second and third belong to the domain of evolutionary biology. All these questions are fundamental in at least two senses: first, they are of great objective, or scientific interest—if we knew the answers to them, then we should be well on the way towards understanding the extraordinary variety of things that go on in the world about us; and secondly, they are of great subjective, or human interest—if we knew the answers to them, then we should be well on the way towards understanding who we are and how we fit into the world about us.

This book is concerned with the origin of humankind. The idea for the book arose out of a public lecture series entitled 'Human Origins', which I organized in Oxford in the autumn of 1984. The aim of the series, which was offered under the auspices of the University of Oxford, Department for External Studies, was to provide an accurate, accessible and up-to-date introduction to the scientific study of human evolution. The task of fulfilling this aim was made all the more easy and enjoyable by the generosity of my Department in providing resources sufficient to enable me to invite contributors from abroad. More-or-less free from the customary constraint of a tight budget, I therefore drew up a short-list of the eight people whom I regarded as ideal representatives of contemporary scientific studies of human origins in front of a general audience. You may imagine my delight when all eight of my 'A Team' agreed to participate in the lecture series!

Human origins follows fairly closely both the pattern and the spirit of the lecture series. The opening talk, by the well-known Oxford evolutionary biologist Richard Dawkins, was impressively wide-ranging: it began with a gripping account of why any theory of human origins must be Darwinian; and it concluded with an intriguing discussion of the nature and evolutionary significance of human purpose. In the interests of clarity and coherence, it has been decided to split this material into two distinct short chapters and to place these at either end of the volume, where they may be regarded as thematic 'book-ends'. Anyone who reads these chapters and still refuses to admit the relevance of Charles Darwin's theory of natural selection to an understanding of human existence must be beyond the reach of rational argument.

In Chapter 2, the anatomist Michael Day brings us almost literally down to earth with an assessment of the most important fossil evidence relating to human origins. It is a remarkable fact that Darwin worked out a great many of the most important features of human evolution with almost no help whatsoever from the fossil record. This, of course, is because fossils are only one of a number of important types of evidence relating to evolution. Michael Day's authoritative review demonstrates at least two things: first, in the century or so since Darwin's death—and often in the face of enormous practical difficulties, palaeoanthropologists have made an astonishingly large number of important fossil finds; and, secondly, these finds are now an essential guide to the formulation of general theories of human origins.

Fossils are the most famous source of clues relating to human origins. By contrast, molecules are altogether less familiar. Yet today, molecular biological studies of proteins and genetic material (DNA) constitute one of the fastest-growing and most impressive branches of evolutionary biology. In Chapter 3 the molecular geneticist Alec Jeffreys explains exactly how a knowledge of the fine structure of genes can be used to reconstruct our family tree. Genetic studies can tell us which among the living primates are our closest living relatives, and how long the human branch has been growing on the tree of primate evolution. Provocatively, Alec Jeffreys suggests that to be consistent with the molecular evidence the chimpanzee and the gorilla should be reclassified with us in the single genus, *Homo*. That this has not yet happened may be as much to do with our anxiety to preserve our own uniqueness as it is to do with our ignorance of the relevant evidence.

Uniquely, the study of human origins is associated with a small number of charismatic figures who, between them, have made a large number of crucial fossil finds. Amongst these figures, none is better known than the Kenyan anthropologist and fossil-hunter Richard Leakey. Following in the footsteps of his pioneering parents, Louis and Mary, Richard Leakey has added greatly to our knowledge of hominid evolution, particularly through his work around the shores of Lake Turkana in northern Kenya. In Chapter 4, he provides a personal overview of recent fossil finds from East Africa, including his own discovery in 1984 of the almost complete skeleton of a boy who lived at the Lake Turkana site approximately 1.6 Ma ago. I still recall vividly the excitement with which we listened to Richard's description of this discovery just a few months after it had been made.

While much of the most widely popularized fossil-hunting has been concerned with the relatively early period during which the hominids diverged from the great apes, equally important work has been going on in much younger geological deposits, with a view to reconstructing the emergence of modern human populations from their immediate ancestors. In Chapter 5, Christopher Stringer assesses the evidence from around the world, bearing on the question of whether modern humans are descended from a single immediate ancestor or several distinct immediate ancestors. His wide-ranging assessment makes it clear that only now, with the coming together of palaeontology and molecular biology, are we at last in a position to answer a question which has exercised anthropologists for almost two hundred years.

Adrienne Zihlman begins Chapter 6 by comparing the investigation of human origins to the solving of a mystery: 'one gathers clues from a wide range of sources, analyses them, and finally puts them together to point to the culprit'. The rest of the chapter is an illustration of just how effective this puzzle-solving approach can be when it comes to answering crucial questions such as: what kind of creature was the last common ancestor of ourselves and the great apes? Combining fossil evidence, molecular biology, and careful comparisons between humans and living apes, Adrienne Zihlman makes a persuasive case for considering the pygmy chimpanzee as a model of the last common ancestor. Her work suggests that we may have a great deal more to learn from pygmy chimpanzees, not only about what the earliest hominids may have looked like, but also about what kind of lives they may have led. Here is yet another good reason for doing everything we can to prevent the extinction of our rare and increasingly threatened relatives.

Glynn Isaac did a splendid job of representing archaeology in our original lecture series, and it was with great sadness that I learnt of his untimely death the following year. Chapter 7 has been reconstructed from the partially edited transcript on which Glynn was working shortly before his death. However imperfectly, I believe that this chapter gives a real sense both of Glynn's enthusiasm for his subject and of his excitement at the coming together of archaeology and ecology in the attempt to reconstruct ancient human environments. Glynn was a pioneer in the quest for a better understanding of the dynamics of human origins. He spurned all simplistic approaches to his subject, and met head-on the very great challenge of piecing together the ways of life of our hominid ancestors from the most painstaking and minute study of ancient living sites and modern savannah ecology. His call to young people considering a career in science to become involved in this indispensable undertaking is perhaps his most fitting epitaph.

In recent years, molecular biology has established an astonishingly high degree of genetic similarity between ourselves and the great apes. How can this genetic similarity be squared with our very great mental superiority over our closest living relatives? In Chapter 8, the psychologist Richard

Passingham cuts a clean swath through the dense undergrowth of speculation that has come to surround this problem. By combining some basic facts about the physical resemblances between ape and human brains, with some equally basic facts about the ways in which apes and humans use their brains, he arrives at a bold, if unromantic, solution. We are smarter than apes, not because we are radically different from them genetically, but because quite small genetic changes triggered the development of a bigger computer (i. e. a larger brain) and better programming methods.

This sober assessment of the mental gap between apes and ourselves paves the way for the final chapter of the book, in which Richard Dawkins reconsiders the problem of human freedom in the light of a Darwinian perspective on human origins. Are we completely bound by the process that made us, or can we transcend this process in a way that marks us out from the rest of the animal kingdom? Richard Dawkins's answer to this question may perhaps come as a surprise to some readers; but I shall not spoil their enjoyment of his argument by anticipating it here.

Our lecture series was a sell-out, and the vast majority of the audience was obviously very appreciative of what it heard. Inevitably, however, there were one or two people who came along simply in order to sling mud at the very idea of an evolutionary perspective on human origins. As chairman, I came to recognize one mud-slinger in particular, for each week he found some pretext or other on which to get up and ask an aggressive 'leading' question. The assumption that appeared to underlie most of his remarks was that since the scientific verdict on this or that aspect of human evolution today was different from the verdict that he had been given several decades ago, then the entire field of study must be totally fraudulent. Nothing, of course, could be further from the truth. To be sure, many of the detailed conclusions concerning our descent from the world of the apes have changed over the years; but this change is a sign of scientific health, not scientific sickness. The fact is that we live in exciting times; in times when not just new finds, but new kinds of finds, are adding substantially to our understanding of human evolution. Inevitably and rightly, therefore, *Human origins* constitutes a snapshot of a fast-moving scene. Something will have gone sadly wrong if, in twenty years' time, we have not got something new to say. In the meantime, I believe that the contributions contained in this book represent some of the best things that can be said today about the fundamental question of why, and how, we came into existence.

J.R.D.

Oxford
1988

Contents

This book is dedicated to the memory of Glynn Isaac, 1937–1985

The editor would like to thank Mrs Barbara Isaac for her assistance with the manuscript on which Glynn Isaac was working at the time of his death. He is also grateful to the staff of the Oxford University Press for help in collecting and collating materials for the book.

Contributors

John R. Durant, Editor

Department for External Studies, University of Oxford, Rewley House, 1 Wellington Square, Oxford OX1 2JA.

Richard Dawkins,

Department of Zoology, University of Oxford, South Parks Road, Oxford.

Michael H. Day,

Department of Anatomy, St. Thomas's Hospital Medical School, Lambeth Palace Road, London SE1 7EH

Glynn Isaac,

Late Professor of Anthropology, Department of Anthropology, Harvard University, Cambridge, Massachusetts 02138, USA

Alec Jeffreys,

Department of Genetics, University of Leicester, Adrian Building, University Road, Leicester LE1 7RH

Richard Leakey,

Director/Chief Executive, National Museums of Kenya, PO Box 40658, Nairobi, Kenya.

Richard Passingham,

Department of Experimental Psychology, University of Oxford, South Parks Road, Oxford.

Christopher B. Stringer,

Department of Palaeontology, British Museum (Natural History), Cromwell Road, London SW7 5BD

Adrienne L. Zihlman,

Department of Anthropology, University of California, Santa Cruz, California 95064 USA

1

Why any study of human origins must be Darwinian*

Richard Dawkins

For me the most interesting problem in the whole of science is the problem of how we came into existence. By 'we', I mean not merely we as human beings but we as animals, as living organisms. This amounts to the problem of how the simple laws of physics, unaided by any supernatural designer, could have given rise to the organized complexity that we call life. It was the great achievement of Charles Darwin to solve this problem once and for all with the theory of natural selection. Darwin believed that his theory could explain how evolution has come about. Today, we have an enormous amount of empirical evidence to show that he was right. But in this chapter, I shall argue something more than that. Natural selection is not just a correct scientific theory of how evolution occurs; it is the only scientific theory that is capable, in principle, of explaining how evolution occurs. That is why any theory of human origins must be Darwinian.

Before Darwin, the organized complexity of life was so overwhelmingly impressive that most people who thought about the problem believed that it must have been intelligently designed by God. If I had lived before Darwin, I would have fallen in with the views of the Reverend William Paley. Here is the famous opening passage from his book *Natural theology* (1802); it is quite long, but it is worth quoting in full as it gives a vivid impression of the force of Paley's argument:

In crossing a heath, suppose I pitched my foot against a stone, and were asked how the stone came to be there; I might possibly answer, that, for any thing I knew to the contrary, it had lain there for ever; nor would it perhaps be very easy to show the absurdity of this answer. But suppose I had found a watch upon the ground, and it should be inquired how the watch happened to be in that place; I should hardly think

*This chapter was, with great pains and skill, transcribed and edited by Dr John Durant from a tape-recording of my lecture in this series, which I myself had not intended for publication. The lecture was delivered during the time that I was writing *The Blind Watchmaker* (Longman, 1986), and there is an inevitable overlap with passages in that book. This does not apply to the material in Chapter 9, which has not been published before.

of the answer which I had before given,—that, for any thing I knew, the watch might have always been there. Yet why should not this answer serve for the watch as well as for the stone? Why is it not as admissible in the second case, as in the first? For this reason, and for no other, viz. that, when we come to inspect the watch, we perceive (what we could not discover in the stone) that its several parts are framed and put together for a purpose, e.g. that they are so formed and adjusted as to produce motion, and that motion is so regulated as to point out the hour of the day . . . This mechanism being observed (it requires indeed an examination of the instrument, and perhaps some previous knowledge of the subject, to perceive and understand it; but being once, as we have said, observed and understood) the inference, we think, is inevitable, that the watch must have had a maker; that there must have existed, at some time, and at some place or other, an artificer or artificers who formed it for the purpose which we find it actually to answer; who comprehended its construction, and designed its use.

Paley's argument depends upon the difference in complexity between a stone and a watch. Stones belong to the world of physics, which is the world of simplicity. Watches and organisms belong to the world of biology, which is the world of almost unimaginable complexity. Complexity is a statistical concept; it means statistical improbability. If we take the parts of a stone and we recombine them randomly in many different ways, we shall find that all the results are nearly the same; the arrangement makes little difference. But if we do the same with a watch, we shall find that of all the ways of scrambling its nuts, bolts, cogs, and springs, only one tells the time. So it is with living organisms. Of all the ways of scrambling the parts of a cactus, only a tiny proportion will live and flower and reproduce themselves.

Living organisms are staggeringly improbable combinations of their component parts. It is worth dwelling on this point a little, since it gives us a feel for the size of the problem that Paley raised and Darwin solved. Take us as an example. In the human body there are about 10^{13} cells. About 10^{10} of these are nerve cells in the brain, which are interconnected with around a hundred-thousand miles of 'wiring'. The retina of the human eye is a bank of photocells, connected to the brain by a multi-way cable. The most elaborate cables that telephone engineers ordinarily deal with have a few dozen or a few hundred wires in them. Each of our two optic nerves is a multi-way cable with about three million wires in it, each carrying a different message independently to the brain.

The astronomer Sir Fred Hoyle is greatly impressed by the staggering improbability of living organisms, which he has attempted to use to refute his own misunderstanding of the theory of natural selection. The chance, he tells us, that even a comparatively simple living organism will come together fully formed from a random assemblage of its component parts, is about the same as the chance that a hurricane blowing through a scrapyard will spontaneously assemble a Boeing 747. So far, of course, he is absolutely right. Of all the possible ways in which the parts of a Boeing 747 could be blown together, only a tiny proportion would fly; and since a house-fly is an even more complicated flying machine than a Boeing 747, the same thing applies to it, and to all other organisms. But the reason why this perfectly valid point is not an argument against Darwinism is that the assembly of organisms by blind chance is not what the theory of natural selection is all about.

To explain what natural selection *is* all about, I want to make a distinction between one-off selection and cumulative selection. One-off selection is the hypothetical process whereby chance alone in a single step produces some desired result—assembling an entire Boeing 747 from scrap, for example, or assembling an entire house-fly from a pile of house-fly cells. In biological terms, one-off selection means a single generation of non-random selection. Cumulative selection is a step-by-step process, in which each step gives rise to the conditions for the next to occur. In biological terms, we have a series of generations, in which each is acted upon by natural selection, and hands on a slightly changed genetic raw material to the next.

The difference between one-off and cumulative selection can be illustrated by means of an analogy with the combination lock on a bank vault. Given a particular lock, it is easy to calculate the chance of somebody spinning the dials at random and opening the lock; it depends on the number of dials and the number of positions on each dial. In the case of bank vault locks, of course, there is a very large number of possible positions for the dials, and it is virtually impossible for a burglar, relying on chance alone, to hit upon the correct combination. This, then, is one-off selection. But suppose now that the burglar is able to twiddle each dial in turn and detect when it is in the right position, perhaps by listening for a distinctive click; and suppose also that as each dial clicks into place, the vault door opens a fraction and a coin falls out. Under these conditions, it is easy to see that the burglar will open the vault very quickly. This is cumulative selection, and the crucial point about it is that each small step is rewarded and provides the basis for the next.

One of the proverbial ways in which improbability is demonstrated is a thought experiment involving monkeys hammering away at random on type-writers. How long, it is asked, will it take them to type the complete works of Shakespeare? I set my computer the task of typing at random—not the complete works of Shakespeare—but just one line. I chose for this purpose an appropriate piece from Hamlet:

HAMLET   :   Do you see yonder cloud that's almost in shape of a camel?
POLONIUS: By the mass, and 'tis like a camel, indeed.
HAMLET   :   Methinks it is like a weasel.
POLONIUS: It is backed like a weasel.
HAMLET   :   Or like a whale?
POLONIUS: Very like a whale.

WDLDMNLTDTJBKWIRZREZLMQCO PS
Y YVMQKZPGJXWVHGLAWFVCHQYOPY
MWR SWTNUXMLCDLEUBXTQHNZVJQF
FU OVAODVYKDGXDEKYVMOGGS VTU
HZQZDSFZIHIVPHZPETPWVOVPMZGF
GEWRGZRPBCTPGQMCKHFDBGW ZCCF

Fig. 1.1. A series of random phrases of the same length as 'Methinks it is like a weasel'. See text for explanation.

Taking the one phrase 'Methinks it is like a weasel', I got the computer to type random phrases of the correct length, until it came up with the correct combination of letters. Some of its efforts are illustrated in Fig. 1.1. Before long I grew bored, and so I did a simple calculation to find out how long I would have to wait. It turned out that I would have to wait a million million million million times as long as the universe has existed for my computer to get the target phrase 'Methinks it is like a weasel' by chance alone. That is Fred Hoyle's problem. I then made it easier for my poor little computer by employing a Darwinian rather than a Fred Hoyle algorithm. What I needed was a process of cumulative selection to replace the one-off selection that would never work. What I did, therefore, was to programme the computer to generate a random parent phrase, breed a hundred random minor variants of it, select whichever one of these was closest to the target phrase as parent of the next generation, breed another hundred random variants of it, and so on. This time, instead of taking a million million million million times the age of the universe, my computer arrived at the target phrase 'Methinks it is like a weasel' in 64 generations, in about twenty minutes. Some of the steps by which it did this are illustrated in Fig. 1.2.

Here, therefore, is the solution to Fred Hoyle's problem. Evolution has produced even the staggering complexity that is you or me, because it has not depended upon one-off selection but rather upon cumulative selection step-by-step across vast intervals of geological time. Cumulative selection really can generate extraordinarily improbable structures, so long as these can be

Y YVMQKSPFTXWSHLIKEFV HQYSPY
YETHINKSPITXISHLIKEFA WQYSEY
METHINKS IT ISSLIKE A WEFSEY
METHINKS IT ISBLIKE A WEASES
METHINKS IT ISJLIKE A WEASED
METHINKS IT IS LIKE A WEASEP

Fig. 1.2. A number of stages through which the phrase 'Methinks it is like a weasel' is generated by cumulative selection. See text for explanation.

achieved gradually through a series of intermediates, each of which is more evolutionarily successful than the one that went before. Of course, there is no target to guide biological evolution, and in this respect my simple computer program is an imperfect, even potentially misleading, model of Darwinian processes. But the point is that Darwinian selection builds organic structures by small stages, in a way that makes statistically improbable end-products not just possible but inevitable. In real life, the criterion for selection is not resemblance to a distant target, but rather survival and hence reproductive success. The qualities that make for reproductive success are— obviously—the qualities that tend to accumulate over the generations.

Having accepted that Darwin's theory really can fulfil its intended purpose, namely explain the organized complexity of life, I want to consider whether the same can be said of its main scientific rivals. I have space to deal with just two of them, Lamarckism and macromutationism. In each case, I shall suggest that, in addition to the evidence against them, there are logical arguments against their being able to explain organized complexity, even in principle. In other words, they are not real rivals to Darwinian selection.

The explanation of evolution that has come to be associated with the name of Lamarck, is a theory of adaptation by instruction. According to this theory, the environment somehow imposes itself upon the organism, so that the goodness-of-fit between organism and environment comes about by direct imprinting from outside. This requires the inheritance of acquired characteristics, and there is no evidence that such inheritance occurs. But I want to make the more radical case that Lamarckism *had* to be wrong in principle. Even if the inheritance of acquired characteristics did occur, as it might in some other life-form elsewhere in the universe, it would not produce the organized complexity that we are trying to explain.

Let us take the hypothetical example of the eye. This, as we have said, is an extremely complex device: it has a lens, an iris diaphragm, a retina, and so on. The lens has exactly the right optical properties, and it is exactly the right distance from the retina to focus a serviceable image. The Darwinian theory has no trouble in explaining the evolution of precise adaptations like these: in a population of animals dependent upon vision for finding food or escaping from predators, even the slightest genetic improvement in the eye may increase an individual's survival and reproductive success. A Lamarckian explanation, however, has to go something like this: in a population of animals with comparatively poor eyes, repeated use of these organs produces optical improvements which are handed on to offspring by the inheritance of acquired characteristics. But how can this Lamarckian mechanism possibly work? Does the flow of light through a lens make it more transparent, or better shaped, or better positioned? Why should mere use improve eyes, when we know that it has exactly the opposite effect on other instruments (except, apparently, violins)?

There are one or two cases, beloved by Lamarckians in the past, in which the principle of improvement through use appears at first sight more plausible. For example, if you use your muscles a lot, they grow bigger and stronger. If you walk around with bare feet a lot, the skin on their soles becomes thicker and tougher. If only acquired characteristics such as these were inherited, it seems that we would improve down the generations. But even here the Lamarckian theory is in trouble, because it has to assume that the acquired characteristics are improvements. Although it is such a familiar fact that we usually take it for granted, it is not obvious why mere exercise of muscles causes them to grow bigger and stronger. They could equally well grow smaller and weaker, and on the face of it you'd think that they would. When a man-made machine has a part that is subject to a lot of wear and tear, it does in fact begin to wear out. The reason why our muscles do not behave in this way is that Darwinian selection has built into them a tendency to respond adaptively to increased use. But that is exactly the point; even in the most superficially favourable cases, Lamarckism has to rely on a Darwinian underpinning to ensure that acquired characteristics are actually improvements. It is for this kind of reason that I think that evolution cannot, in principle, be Lamarckian. It has to be Darwinian.

The second supposed alternative to Darwinism that I shall deal with is macromutationism. Before doing so, however, I want to make two very important distinctions. The first is between macromutationism and punctuated equilibrium. If you have acquired your knowledge of evolution from The *Sunday Times*, The *Observer*, or the BBC, you will have been under the impression that Darwinism has been rocked to its foundations in the past few years, by a new theory called punctuated equilibrium. This is nonsense. If the theory of punctuated equilibrium is true, then it is no more than a very minor gloss on Darwinism. Figure 1.3 compares the traditional method with this newer way of representing how evolution occurs a large scale. According to the traditionalists, an evolutionary trend towards, say, larger size, is represented as a gradual change over time; according to the proponents of punctuated equilibrium, animals stay very much the same size for long periods of time, and then switch abruptly to either a smaller or a larger size, during so-called 'speciation events'.

This difference seems clear enough, but everything depends on what we suppose is going on at speciation events. A careful reading of the more cautious statements of those who support punctuated equilbrium reveals that these events are episodes of perfectly ordinary Darwinian evolution, albeit telescoped into very short bursts of rapid change sandwiched between very long periods of no change at all. In effect, then, what is new about punctuated equilibria is not the punctuations but the equilibria: the injection into evolutionary history of long periods of stagnation when nothing much happens. Darwin would not have found that at all remarkable. As he himself

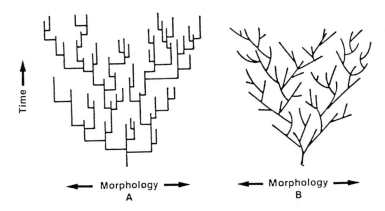

Fig. 1.3 The theory of punctuated equilibrium, *A*, compared with the traditional way of representing evolution on a large scale, *B*.

put it: 'The periods during which species have been undergoing modification, though very long as measured in years, have probably been short in comparison with the periods during which these same species remained without undergoing change'.

This is the modest theory of punctuated equilibria. But we must be careful to distinguish it from the far more ambitious theory of macromutation. A macromutation is a short, sharp genetic shock; a single big change that occurs in one generation. It is the sort of thing that might make a son so different from his father that he would be classed as another species. The idea that such macromutations play a major part in evolution is sometimes subscribed to, and it has been defended by some of the proponents of punctuated equilibria; hence the confusion between two things which are in reality quite distinct.

Having distinguished between punctuated equilibria and macromutationism, I now want to distinguish between two forms of macromutationism itself, which I shall call '747 macromutationism' and 'stretched DC8 macromutationism'. Both theories involve very large mutations. In both cases sons are radically different from their fathers. The 747 macromutations get their name from Fred Hoyle's story about the scrapyard. A 747 macromutation would be something like the one-off invention of an eye—iris diaphragm, lens, retina, the lot—from bare skin. Obviously, 747 macromutations are impossible for the statistical reasons that we discussed earlier. If somebody could produce cast-iron evidence for the existence of 747 macromutations, I would cease to believe in Darwinism and I would start to believe in God. But the evidence would have to be very good, and I would have to be sure that the macromutations weren't really of the stretched DC8 variety instead.

A stretched DC8 macromutation is not impossible. The stretched DC8 was an airliner modelled on an earlier one, the ordinary DC8. It was simply an ordinary DC8 made a bit longer. Macromutations in living organisms can be of this form. They can be changes of a very large magnitude that do not involve the introduction of new organized complexity. A stretched DC8 has no more organized complexity than an ordinary DC8; it just has certain bits of organized complexity enlarged or repeated. Similarly, a giraffe's neck has no more organized complexity than an antelope's; it just goes on a bit longer. If the giraffe's neck had shot out from some ancestral short-necked ancestor in a single step, that would be a stretched DC8 macromutation. It would have been rather remarkable to witness, of course; but it would not have been a miracle, because all the necessary organized complexity—vertebrae, nerves, blood vessels, and so on—was already there to begin with.

Examples of stretched DC8 macromutations are well known in the fruit fly: *Drosophila melanogaster*. They are very striking. One can observe mutant flies with a complete leg growing out of a socket where an antenna should be. Everything about the leg is correct, but it is a leg and not an antenna and it is in the wrong place. This is a mutation of very large effect, but it does not violate the laws of probability in the way that a 747 macro-mutation would, because the instructions for making the leg are already in the fly. All that has happened is that these instructions have been carried out in the wrong place.

When Darwin insisted that evolution is gradual, I think that he meant that it is not of the '747 type'. For example, he wrote, 'If it could be demonstrated that any complex organ existed which could not possibly have been formed by numerous slight modifications, my theory would absolutely break down'. On the other hand, I don't think that Darwin really minded whether or not on occasion evolution was of the stretched DC8 type. 'About sudden jumps', he wrote to a correspondent in 1860, 'I have no objection to them—they would aid me in some cases. All I can say is, that I went into the subject, and found no evidence to make me believe in jumps; and a good deal pointing in the other direction'. It was where 747-type jumps were being discussed that Darwin was passionately against them. He was faced by critics who wanted to believe in 747 macromutations for plainly theological reasons, invoking the creator at crucial nodal points in the evolutionary process. That was what Darwin rejected. It is what all Darwinists—all reasonable people—must reject.

2

Fossil Man: the hard evidence

Michael Day

Introduction

The title I have chosen has several possible meanings. Perhaps the most obvious is that the aspect of human evolution which I shall discuss concerns physical objects rather than theory. Then again, anatomists sometimes differentiate tissues as being either hard, like bones and teeth, or soft, like muscle. Finally, the title could be taken to mean that the evidence we shall be considering in this chapter is difficult to accept or interpret. I leave readers to choose their own interpretation of the title.

Fossil bones are the preserved evidence, in geological deposits, of former animal populations, and populations is a word that I would like to emphasize straight away. In the history of our subject—and even today—people talk of one fossil having given rise to another, or of one fossil being descended from another. This is not a very realistic proposition. We should always try to think and speak in terms of populations, even though this is not an easy thing to do. Thinking in terms of populations immediately raises the paradox of the sample. One of the accusations that is often levelled at those of us who look at fossil bones is: 'You only have very small amounts of material to deal with and to examine, and therefore your conclusions are not very reliable'. If we think of the sample in terms of the possible populations from which it may have been drawn, then the answer is 'yes'—we do have an extremely small sample to work with. On the other hand, if we look through the British Museum catalogues of fossil hominids, which run into several volumes, then we find that there are now some thousands of specimens, world-wide, which comprise the total of the hard evidence. On the one hand, we have almost too much to cope with, but on the other hand, we are, on occasion, guilty of extrapolating from small samples. In our defence, it is true that electron microscopists will examine very few cells and base their theories on those cells that they have examined, which are necessarily a very small sample of the total number that may have been available. Their opportunities for repeated sampling, however, are somewhat greater than ours.

One of the major preoccupations of palaeoanthropologists is classification: the way in which the biologist attempts to bring order into the chaos of the natural world by grouping animals and plants with similar features. The principal classificatory system that is used is the Linnaean system. This system is based on similarity, and it was originally intended for use with living forms. But it was obvious that once the living forms were classified, fossil forms would have to come into the picture too; after all, a Pleistocene hippopotamus really looks very much like a modern one, and certainly wouldn't be confused with a lion. Hence, Linnaean taxonomy has come to have a palaeontological or historical value, as well as a neontological or contemporary value. The application of this system over the years has produced a view of the past, based on distinctions between different 'grades' of animal life.

Another approach to the problem of classification in recent years has been that of the German taxonomist Willi Hennig. Hennig's system relies upon differentiating groups of creatures by the first appearance of morphological features in the fossil record. It discounts features that are shared by populations that are more ancient than the one under consideration. New features are said to indicate points of divergence, where the fossil record might allow us to detect diversifying evolution or 'cladogenetic' change, as opposed to successive evolution, or 'anagenetic' change.

Interestingly enough, in neither Linnaean (or 'gradist') nor Hennigian (or 'cladist') classification, would the proponents claim that the dating of the find under consideration is of any importance whatsoever; rather the requirements of morphological analysis are the only things that count. Despite this, I must confess that I have never met a palaeoanthropologist who was totally uninterested in the dating of a fossil with which he was presented. At the very least, it's a comfort when your morphological assessment seems to match with the dating that the geologists or geochronologists have given. The gradists and the cladists have clashed in recent years, but in human evolutionary studies it is becoming clear that a purely cladistic approach is unsatisfactory at the level of taxonomic differentiation between genera and species. The very idea of 'ancestry' becomes questionable if a new feature or group of features excludes relationship. On the other hand, pure gradists may have to provide explanations for apparent reversals within the fossil record (e.g. australopithecines have a thin skull, but *Homo erectus* has a thick skull, yet the skull of *Homo sapiens* is again thin). Other preoccupations of palaeoanthropologists are dental, masticatory, and locomotor. These systems provide data that tell us about diet and mode of progression. All are important in trying to obtain an understanding of the life economy of the group, and all are contributory factors in taxonomic analysis.

The first chapter of this book introduced Darwinism. Simply put, a pool of variability, acted upon by cumulative natural selection has led to what is known as Darwinian evolution; in popular terms, the survival of the fittest (not the most physically fit). Darwinian fitness may be genetic, but it may also be expressed as the 'fit' of the individual, the population, and the species to the environment. A close fit of an animal to its ecological situation, its 'econiche' as the Americans call it, is a form of specialism, and specialism is one route to survival. But there is a pitfall—that of environmental change. If a creature is highly specialized—and thus closely fitted to its environment—and the environment changes, then the creature may become extinct. Generalism is the specialism of primates. Progressive primates are opportunistic; they are adaptable, and hence able and willing to change in response to changing environments.

Evolutionary change is directional and usually has a measurable rate. Evolution is a continuous and continuing process leading to a detectable shift in the means or (average appearances) of characters of populations through time. The time factor is important and is implicit in the usage of the word 'evolution', which commonly means a slow change as opposed to a rapid change or revolution. But evolutionary rates vary between and within evolving species, and these varying rates are currently of great interest. As Richard Dawkins has already explained in Chapter 1, traditional 'gradualism' has recently been assailed by the 'punctuated equilibrists', if I can call them that, who would attempt to explain the fossil record rather differently from the way that Darwin did.

Darwin believed evolution to be continuous and gradual, and he tended to explain gaps in the fossil record as 'missing evidence'. The 'punctuated equilibrists' do not see evolution as continuous and gradual, and they believe that, in the evolution of many species, long periods of stasis are punctuated by periods of rapid evolution. They regard gaps in the fossil record as evidence of very rapid change with little time for sampling—for them the gaps are evidence of rapid change. This general discussion has been brought into the study of human origins, and the fossil record of our own ancestry has been cited as a good example of punctuated evolution. Certainly, there are several well-recognized stages in the process of human evolution: the australopithecines, or ape-man; the hominines, or first true men; and the sapiens, or modern men. However, there are many intermediate forms showing the signs of mosaic evolution to a greater or lesser degree, and the increasing number of finds seems to add year by year to the elimination of the gaps between these major stages.

Evolution and the hominids: the major groups

When we come to look at the hard evidence, there are many ways of tackling the problem. One is simply to treat the subject historically, beginning with the Gibraltar skull found in 1848, and working our way through to Richard Leakey's latest find. However, this is not necessarily the way which will give us the best understanding of the current state of the subject. The history of discovery has not been chronological in an evolutionary sense, since of course it has been totally opportunistic. The distribution of fossils, for example, equates very well with the distribution of collectors; and we have rather more fossils that are relatively recent than we have of those that are very ancient, simply because the more recent ones have not had such a long time in which to disintegrate. Therefore the fossil record that we have is, at any given time, bound to be incomplete, and yet it has presented the challenge of interpretation to successive generations of palaeoanthropologists. It is worth remembering, also, that these palaeoanthropologists can only observe and compare those things that have been preserved—bones, skulls, jaws, and teeth for the most part; but also, and more recently, footprints. Footprints have been discovered in various cave sites in France, as well as in more than one site from East Africa. These footprints provide evidence of soft tissue and of function, in terms of the way in which particular creatures stood and walked; they are an exciting new source of information on Early Man.

At this point, it may be useful to introduce what I call the 'mushroom theory' of human evolution. This is an attempt to express, in both time and space, something of the general arrangement of the fossil record (Fig. 2.1). There are names there that are probably familiar: the australopithecines, the hominines, and, of course, the sapiens. There are also names that are perhaps less familiar: the afarines, for example, which I shall discuss later. The point of the diagram is to show that there are periods of population expansions, and there are also periods when change seems to have taken place relatively rapidly. Overlaps, both in time and space, also occur, because populations evolve at differential rates and in differing geographical centres. The process is, however, gradual, and many intermediate forms are known. Let us now consider the hard evidence relating to each of the major groups of fossil hominids.

The australopithecines

What then of the real hard evidence? In 1985 January we celebrated the diamond jubilee of the find of the Taung infant skull by Raymond Dart in 1925. It is appropriate that we should pay tribute to Raymond Dart. Dart was the man who first recognized the little skull that came from a limestone quarry in South Africa (Fig. 2.2). At first glance, it appears to have many ape-like features, such as the protruding jaw. However, it has a rather bulging forehead, and the size of its brain (as judged by an endocast of rock which was inside) is larger than it should be for a creature of that age if it were simply a kind of chimpanzee. The teeth also show some extremely interesting details, although these were not at first recognized by Dart because they were

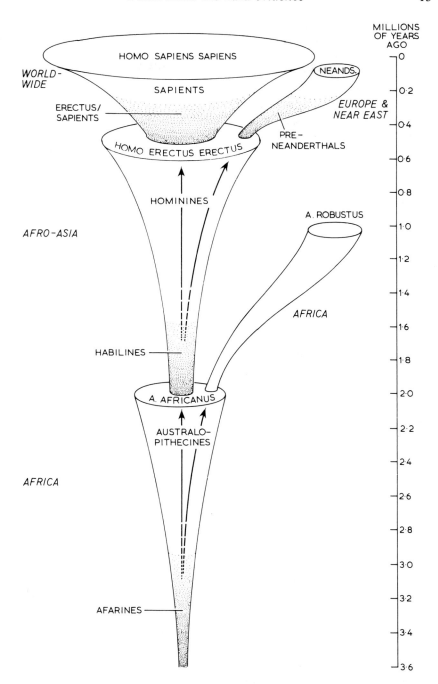

Fig. 2.1. The "mushroom" theory.

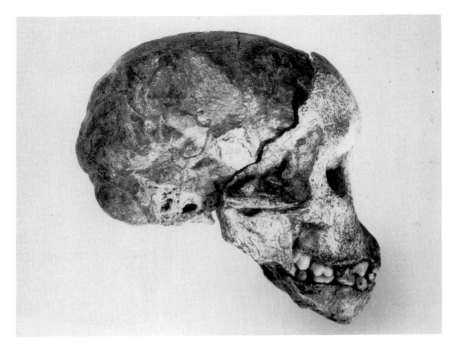

Fig. 2.2.   The Taung infant skull. Right-lateral view. Photograph A.R. Hughes.

all obscured by matrix. When Dart brought the Taung skull to London, the anatomical establishment was highly sceptical. Grafton Elliott-Smith and others simply dismissed it—because it was juvenile, it was incomplete, and there was insufficient evidence to suggest that it was a hominid, or man-like creature.

It was some years before confirmation came in the form of new finds from other sites. For example, Robert Broom discovered a skull in the limestone caves of Sterkfontein in South Africa. Limestone caves commonly form when water percolates through the ground, and then the resulting caverns open to the outside. Animals may find their way into such caves and die, and become incorporated in the material, or breccia, that accumulates on their floors. The Sterkfontein skull, when it was removed and cleaned, proved to be extremely interesting. The upper jaw was projecting (or prognathic), but the skull was very rounded and the plane at the back of the neck, to which the neck muscles were attached, was arranged in such a way that the balance point was well forward. This indirect evidence indicates that the poise of the head was such that the animal spent a good deal of its time upright on two feet. A little later, pelvic evidence confirmed that the australopithecines—as

Dart called them—walked in a way more similar to modern humans than to modern monkeys and apes. So now it was quite clear that Dart's Taung find was not a freak; it had to be explained.

A second group of australopithecines come from Swartkrans and Kromdraai, and these are much more robust creatures. The teeth are very big, and in order to make large teeth work properly you must have big muscles. If you are unfortunate enough not to have a very large brain, you don't have a very big brain case; therefore you don't have very much room on which to hang those big muscles. Thus it is necessary to make use of bony crests; and that is why creatures like gorillas and chimpanzees have crests on the top of their heads. Some hominids have crests on top of their heads, and also extremely heavy facial buttressing to dissipate the forces of chewing through the face to the cranium. In the robust australopithecines there is an extraordinary size ratio between the small teeth at the front and the large teeth at the back. The teeth at the front—the incisors and canines—are extremely small; behind them are the two premolars; and then behind them are the molars, and these are veritable millstones—they are enormous crushing and grinding teeth. Modern techniques have been used on these specimens. In particular, scanning electron microscopy has told us a great deal about the way in which these teeth were used, by revealing their wear patterns. The dentition of the robust group is quite different from that of the lighter-boned, more gracile australopithecines that come from the same region. Probably the two groups were adapted to quite different ways of life. One of the most important features in the early human evolutionary story is the geography of Plio-Pleistocene East Africa. That geography is now explained by the geological theory of plate tectonics, according to which the Earth's crust is composed of a number of moving plates. The area of East Africa and Saudi Arabia, the Red Sea, and the Gulf of Aden, is a classical example of a triple junction between crustal plates that are moving apart from one another. One plate boundary has been filled by the Red Sea, another goes out of the Gulf of Aden, and a third is represented by the parallel faults of the Great Rift Valley of East Africa. To imagine such a valley, you have to bear in mind that it is a trench which is 64 km (40 miles) across and approximately 610 m (2000 feet) deep. This trench is a line of weakness in the Earth's crust associated with volcanic activity, and there are lakes in its floor. These lakes very often have had volcanic ash rained into them, and thus they are frequently alkaline. This is important, because alkaline conditions are necessary for the preservation of bones.

At the upper end of the Rift Valley, in the region of the Hadar Triangle in Ethiopia, the American palaeoanthropologist Donald Johanson and his team, as well as some French workers, have been recovering some extraordinary hominid fossils in recent years. The most spectacular of all these finds is the famous 'Lucy', which, until recently, was the most complete skeleton of a fossil hominid anywhere in the world. Lucy is remarkable in many ways. She is a partial skeleton, including representatives of almost all the limb bones; we have a shoulder joint, an elbow, a wrist, a hip joint, a knee joint, an ankle joint, and also part of the pelvis. Dated at about 3 million years (Ma) before present (BP), Lucy undoubtedly stood upright, walked, and ran about. We have some hand and toe bones, and at the moment there is a debate about whether or not some of the features of these bones disclose more of an ability to climb trees than other, later, fossil hominids. The question is, did Lucy actually live in trees, or are her arboreal features the vestiges of an ancestor which had rather more arboreal adaptations than she did?

South of the Hadar Triangle is Lake Turkana: an ancient Pleistocene lake whose sediments contain fossils. The modern lake is surrounded by areas of exposure where fossils are 'floating', as it were, to the surface, because the deposits are gradually being eroded by high winds and occasional flash floods. Imagine walking along the dried-up bed of a river and finding in a hole in the bank a skull that is totally undisturbed, its eyes clogged up with mud. Cleaned up, the skull is clearly recognizable as a robust australopithecine. Although there are no teeth, it has a crest on the top of the head, a rather restricted cranial capacity, and heavy buttressing of the cheek area; all this evidence points to the fact that such a creature would have had a heavy jaw, as well as heavy teeth (Fig. 2.3).

Fig. 2.3.   KNM-ER 406. A robust australopithecine skull from Koobi Fora, Kenya. Courtesy of the Director of the National Museums of Kenya.

Skull ER 406 was one of the first that came from East Africa, and it confirmed the fact that the australopithecines were not confined exclusively to the south. Also in East Africa, of course, but a little further south down the Rift Valley, is the famous Olduvai Gorge. It was at Olduvai Gorge in the 1950s and 1960s that Mary and Louis Leakey made their greatest finds. Olduvai Hominid 5, for example, is a robust australopithecine of extreme importance, possibly the best of all the robust australopithecine skulls found. The exciting thing about its discovery is that this skull was the first australopithecine to be securely dated. The South African sites are extremely difficult to date, mainly because our absolute dating methods do not work very well in the limestone deposits there. At Olduvai, however, the volcanic deposits are datable by the potassium/argon radiometric dating technique, and this reveals that Hominid 5, and others with it, lived there at approximately 1.75 Ma BP. In the early 1960s, this date was virtually unbelievable, and still today it gives us pause for thought. Hominid 5 has extremely small canine teeth, and these and other dental features indicate that it is much more similar to humans than to the modern great apes.

Fairly close to Olduvai there is another site called Laetoli, which is one of the world's oldest known hominid sites. The date there is around 3.6 Ma BP—a little bit older than the Hadar site, and the material is, of necessity, becoming rather sparse; but there are two jaws from creatures initially believed by Mary Leakey to belong to a very early form of the genus *Homo*. The question of the taxonomy of these and related East African finds has been a source of interest and argument for many, many years. All kinds of opinions have been put forward, but none of them has been universally accepted. Some commentators have argued that all the robust australopithecines are male and all the gracile ones are female; some have suggested that the two forms are differing species within the same genus *Australopithecus*; and some have held that the two forms are generically distinct. (On this last view, the robust hominids would be placed in a separate genus *Paranthropus*, and the gracile ones would remain in the genus *Australopithecus*.) So the state of classification of the australopithecines is still as much in flux as it ever was.

On top of all this, we now have Johanson's Hadar finds to contend with. Johanson has suggested that his material is older than all of the South African material and, indeed, virtually as old as that from Laetoli. He has lumped the Hadar and Laetoli finds together in what is now known as *Australopithecus afarensis*. Not all palaeoanthropologists accept this step, because some of the material from Hadar is distinctly different from 'Lucy' (for example, it is a very great deal larger). The response of Johanson and his supporters to this point has been the suggestion that 'Lucy' and her 'family' represent an extremely sexually dimorphic species, in which the males are very big in comparison with the females. This may be true, but it is worth pointing out that if it is, then *Australopithecus afarensis* has a wider range of sexual dimorphism than almost any other known primate. It may be right, but it *is* special pleading; and Johanson and his supporters are therefore under a certain amount of pressure on this point. Finally, it has been claimed that the creatures Johanson classifies as *Australopithecus afarensis* are the same as those at Laetoli, and that together these constitute the stem form—the ultimate hominid ancestor of us all. Several scenarios have been offered as to how precisely this may have occurred. One suggestion is that *A. afarensis* gave rise to *A. africanus*, which in turn gave rise to *Homo*; and another that *A. africanus* was a dead end. Debates about these alternatives are likely to be with us for some time to come.[1]

The unique thing about Laetoli is its record of hominid footprints in volcanic ash preserved for over 3.5 million years. This record was an extraordinary find, and, like most good things in science, it occurred by chance when a 'pavemented' area was uncovered by simply brushing away the soil. What seems to have happened is this: a volcano called Sadiman erupted, and rather like Mount St Helens it spewed out showers of volcanic ash, which settled, over a period of some months. Six separate layers have been identified, and two of them are closely associated with raindrop spatters. Clearly, raindrops wetted the ash; and a great variety of animals then proceeded to tramp all over it. Preserved in the ash, to this very day, are the tracks of easily recognizable animals such as giraffes, hippopotamuses, and baboons; but in addition there are the tracks of creatures which have long-since disappeared. For example, there is a lovely track made by the three-toed horse (*Hipparion*). An adult is walking, and then behind it, weaving in and out its footsteps, is the smaller track of a three-toed foal.

Most exciting of all the tracks are those of the hominids. In Fig. 2.4 the single track on the left is smaller than that on the right, and it is possible to see the way in which the heel is dug down and the toes are arranged. We can see that the feet are turned out, and, since the distance between the heel prints can be measured, we can even estimate the stride. There is a known relationship between the stride and foot length, and this gives us an idea of height. These were not very tall individuals, something of the order of about 3'6'' to 4'0''. At first glance the right track appears strange; but closer examination reveals that there are, in fact, two individuals walking and not one. The larger individual is walking in front, and then inside that print is a smaller print. So there

Since this text was prepared the discovery of WT 17000, from West Turkana, Kenya, has added a new dimension to the debate. WT 17000 is a robust australopithecine skull with a tiny brain and huge flaring crests on its head from deposits that are given as 2.5 million years BP. It confirms that robust australopithecines were not specialized *end* products of their evolutionary line but occurred early. This may also push back in time the split between the robust and non robust lines and give weight to those who suggest that there were two species at that time and not one *A. afarensis* stem form.

Fig. 2.4. The Laetoli footprints.

were three individuals in all: the largest, perhaps the father, in front; the mother, slightly smaller, behind; and the child at their side. (I have no evidence whatsoever for making those sex or age attributions other than their relative sizes.) The real point is that they are sophisticated bipeds and sophisticated bipedalism at 3.5 million years is amazing. Comparative photogrammetric analyses with modern human prints of similar character show them to be almost identical in the way in which weight and force is transmitted through the foot to the ground in a bipedal progression.

These, then, are the early Plio-Pleistocene hominid groups that we have to contend with. As we have seen, there are several more-or-less distinct groups; and there are considerable difficulties involved in determining their interrelationships. Frustratingly, the fossil material is no help to those of us who are interested in the origins of bipedalism, because the bipedalism appears in the record almost fully developed. We also have masticatory and dental evidence which gives us some idea of the diet of early hominids; this appears to have been heavy and coarse, and to have required a great deal of crushing, using teeth of large size.

The hominines

In 1890, the Dutchman Eugene Dubois recovered the Java calotte (skull cap). It was the earliest of the *Homo erectus* finds, and interesting in historical terms on its own account. A femur or thigh bone was found very near it, and this has interested me a great deal, because, although the dating of the calotte is probably fairly secure at about 400 000 years BP, the dating of the femur is by no means secure. Moreover, the anatomy of the femur is not what one would expect. Dubois called his find *Pithecanthropus erectus*, on the basis of the modern human features of the femur. It doesn't seem surprising to me that the femur is so modern, because in my opinion it *is* a modern human femur that has been there perhaps for only 175 000 years. X-ray micro-analyses of the calotte and the femur are being performed at present, and these promise to dislodge the femur, at least, from the Middle Pleistocene fossil record.

The Peking *Homo erectus* material is famous for the fact that it was lost during the war, but not before its features were well described. The Middle Pleistocene *Homo erectus* has a bigger brain, a slightly less prognathic jaw, dental features which are rather more advanced than the australopithecines, and a more gracile face (the heavy buttressing of earlier forms has been reduced a good deal). Fortunately, other examples of *Homo erectus* have now been recovered. Thus, a specimen has recently been obtained from Hexian in the Republic of China. There are other examples from East Africa (Olduvai Hominid 9) at one million years, and several other examples from North Africa. There is also half a hip bone which comes from Olduvai Gorge (OH 28). This bone has a rather peculiar buttress arrangement in order to make the pelvis tilt in the distinctive way that it does during bipedal walking. The tilt mechanism is worked through the buttress and the fulcrum of the hip-joint, with muscles attached to the thigh bone below. I suggested some time ago that this tilt mechanism might conceivably be peculiar to *Homo erectus*, because the femur that occurred with it was very much like the femur from Peking. Since then, other finds of similar appearance have confirmed this idea. For example, Richard Leakey's discovery of *Homo erectus* at Koobi Fora in Kenya matches the earlier finds from Peking and Olduvai (Fig. 2.5). KNM-ER 3733 has a number of features about it that resemble those from Peking, but it is rather more gracile. Also found at Koobi Fora, however, was another of those hip bones, and, to my delight, the characteristic buttress feature turned up again. So we now have two examples which, although perhaps not specifically diagnostic for *Homo erectus*, certainly do show that *Homo erectus* had these unusual features.

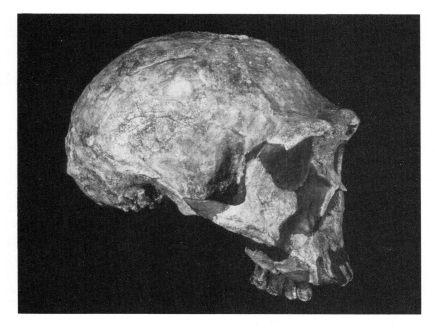

Fig. 2.5. KMR-ER 3733. A *Homo erectus* skull from Koobi Fora, Kenya. Courtesy of the Director of the National Museums of Kenya.

Homo erectus was an upright and bipedal species, of course; and it was widely distributed: from China and Java to North and East Africa. Whether or not there are any true specimens of *Homo erectus* from Europe, is once again a matter for debate. European finds such as the Heidelberg jaw have been attributed to *Homo erectus*, but gradually the record of *Homo erectus* in Europe is being questioned. It is possible that all those specimens that have been attributed to *Homo erectus* in Europe may simply be pre-Neanderthalers. The Bilzingsleben skull, however, has many *Homo erectus* features.

The sapients

The last major fossil group to consider are the Neanderthalers. They were first found in 1856, and in general they have been seen as a highly specialized group adapted to a cold climate. A great deal has been said and written about the Neanderthalers, but it is really only in the past ten years that the true Neanderthaler's features have been identified. These relate to the centre of the face. The centre of the Neanderthaler's face looks as though the whole thing has been grabbed and pulled forward; the face is inflated, and there is a characteristic gap behind the last molar tooth (the retromolar space). There are other details like the bump at the back of the skull, and the fact that the skull appears somewhat inflated in posterior view. The Neanderthalers seem to be a fairly distinct group, and they occur fairly late in our story, but of course the last group of all is *Homo sapiens sapiens*, the group to which we belong.

Evolution and hominids: the intermediate stages

Where have we got to in terms of our mushroom theory (Fig. 2.1)? We have seen that somewhere between 3.5 and 1 Ma BP there are two principal groups of material to explain. These groups belong to the species *Australopithecus africanus* and *Australopithecus robustus*. The robust group became extinct at about 1 Ma BP. We have also seen that from somewhere around 1.5 Ma there appeared a larger group, which we will call *Homo erectus erectus*; and that from this group, about a quarter of a million years ago, there finally emerged *Homo sapiens fossilis* (to use an archaic term). Of course, we also have the Neanderthalers to fit in; most people would derive the Neanderthalers from a *Homo erectus* source. But what of the intermediate stages between these major groups? The intermediate stages are indicated in Fig. 2.1 by the shaded areas at the base of each 'mushroom'. These areas tend to be of particular interest, since they represent periods of progressive evolution from one type to another. Let us consider the possible intermediates at each of the points of evolutionary progression in the fossil record.

The Afarines

The first candidate intermediates are the Afarines, by which I mean the material from Afar and Laetoli that has been attributed to *A. afarensis*. As we have seen, this material is variable; and it may be transitional between a hominoid ancestor and the true hominids. Then again, it may also represent two populations, the smaller members of which may be ancestral to *A. africanus* (or even synonymous with it), while the larger are ancestral to *A. robustus (Paranthropus robustus)* and *A. boisei*.

The habilines

Another intermediate group may exist in between the australopithecines and *Homo erectus*. In the 1960s, Louis Leakey, John Napier, and Phillip Tobias caused a sensation by suggesting that the material from Olduvai which was not from the big robust australopithecine, belonged to a new species of man, *Homo habilis*. This name had been suggested by Raymond Dart, and it means 'able' or 'handy'. Dart suggested the name because hand and foot remains were found at the same time. The Olduvai *Homo habilis* skull was not very well preserved. However, its cranial capacity was larger than that of an australopithecine of roughly the same size, and smaller than that of *Homo erectus*. In addition, other dental features were so advanced that some anatomists said that it really ought to be called *Homo erectus*.

The really exciting fact about *Homo habilis* was that we had found a foot and a hand, which is very rare. The hands and the feet are of great interest to those of us who are interested in locomotion, because it is the business end of the limb which usually has the special features. The rest of the limb can be regarded as a series of joints which enables it to be placed somewhere; but once the limb is in place, it is the hand or the foot that must dig, grasp, hang, or whatever. The hand is a generalized appendage (we have five fingers, but so do lizards). The foot, by contrast, is a very highly specialized organ. We have only to contemplate our big toes to realize what marvellously specialized

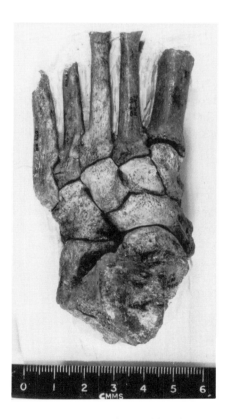

Fig. 2.6. The original articulation of the Olduvai foot by the author, 1960.

objects they are; without them, we would have great difficulties in walking, running, or jumping.

I was privileged to reconstruct the Olduvai foot, and it left me absolutely astonished (Fig. 2.6). To see why, we have to put ourselves back again into the climate of opinion of the 1960s. At that time, no one imagined that these creatures could conceivably be truly bipedal. Rather, it was thought that perhaps they crept around at 45 degrees, or even ran about on all fours. Thus, the fact that they were competently bipedal came as a total shock. However, there can be no doubt about it. When we look at the foot in Fig. 2.6, it is immediately obvious that it is a propulsive organ which does not have the ability to grasp; instead, it has the ability to push force and weight through it in a non-prehensile way. Clearly, the toes and bits of the heel are missing. Clearly, too, there are details of this foot that are different from ours; but even those who have argued a great deal about these anatomical differences are now saying that this foot is capable of true bipedalism. This is what we should expect, since the date of the foot is 1.75 Ma BP, and we now have bipedal footprints at 3.5 Ma BP.

I shall not go into detail about the *Homo habilis* hand, other than to say that some features of the wrist and the top of the thumb indicate that it was

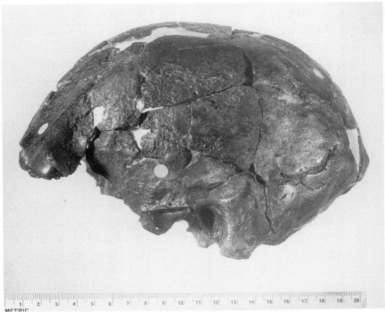

Fig. 2.7.   The Omo II skull from Ethiopia. A *Homo erectus/sapiens* transitional with features of both species in its anatomy but perhaps more of *Homo erectus*.

capable of grasping an object. Certainly, it was quite capable of making the stone tools that were found in association with it.

So here were a skull, a foot, and a hand with an impressive combination of man-like characteristics. It was these characteristics that Tobias claimed were enough to justify placing *Homo habilis* in the genus *Homo*. This claim is once again under discussion because of that most interesting specimen from Koobi Fora, ER 1470; 1470's brain is not like that of an australopithecine; it is quite well expanded. However, it had rather large teeth; and there are other features about the skull which make one feel that it is an intermediate between the australopithecines and *Homo erectus*.

Some workers have classified 1470 as *Homo habilis*; but the question of whether this material will stand up to close analysis and comparison with the other habiline material from Olduvai is still very open.

The erectus/sapiens *transitionals*

Let us consider now the transition between *Homo erectus* and *Homo sapiens*. A skull from the Omo region of Ethiopia (Omo II), one of Richard Leakey's finds, is particularly fascinating. Its cranial capacity is well up to virtually modern standards, but the slope of the forehead and the nuchal plane show it to be very archaic in many ways (Fig. 2.7). Is it *erectus*, or is it modern? A second skull was found with it (Omo I), supposedly of the same age; but the reconstruction shows them to be quite different in many ways (Fig. 2.8). Are the two skulls from the same species? At first, I felt that the only comment that one could make was that they seemed to be at the extremes of the range encompassed within *Homo sapiens*. But on later consideration, and notwithstanding the dating, Chris Stringer and I think that they are distinguishable at least in grade, if not in clade. Thus, these and other similar finds may help to bridge the gap between *erectus* and *sapiens*.

The pre-Neanderthalers

Lastly, the Arago skull from the Pyrenees is another transitional fossil. The Arago finds are dated at 400 000 years BP. Interestingly, these finds include a hip bone. Of the other hip bones, ER 3228 is dated at 1.9 Ma and OH 28 at 700 000 years BP; yet significantly the morphological details of these hip bones seem to me to be very similar. If a group of features of this kind can persist for as long as perhaps a million years, then this might be termed a 'morphological punctuation event'. Whatever success ER 3228 had attained in terms of gait 1.9 Ma ago, there seems to have been no reason to change the way that it worked for over a million years.

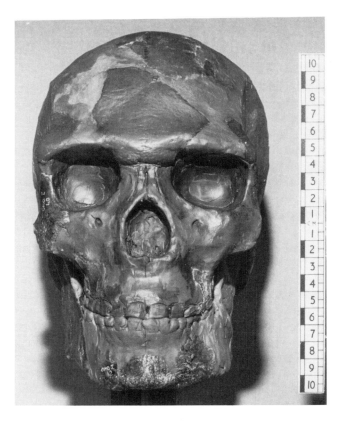

Fig. 2.8.   A new reconstruction of Omo I by the author and Christopher Stringer. Another *Homo erectus/sapiens* transitional, from the same site as Omo II, showing archaic features but more that recall *Homo sapiens* than *Homo erectus*.

Conclusion

This has been a selective survey; there are lots of other sites and finds that could have been mentioned. The debates about all of these sites and finds have gone on for a long time, and I think that they will continue for a long time to come. Is *A. afarensis*, for example, one species or several? Is *Homo erectus* going to be squeezed out by those who are bringing the *Homo erectus/sapiens* transitionals back in time and *Homo habilis* forwards? The evolution of modern man from a series of primate and hominid ancestors is not now in doubt amongst serious students; but the details of that evolution—the precise steps that it followed, the mechanisms that drove it forward, and so on—require further investigation. The hard evidence demands cogent explanations; and in the end, these will surely be forthcoming.

3

Molecular biology and human evolution

Alec J. Jeffreys

Introduction

Most of the characteristics of an organism, ranging from its biochemistry and physiology, to its development, morphology, and behaviour, are crucially affected by its genes. All evolutionary changes ultimately arise from changes in genes; that is, in changes in the detailed structure and organization of DNA within chromosomes. DNA is a long, chain-like molecule that is capable of storing information as a linear sequence of the four nucleotide bases A, C, G, and T. Furthermore, the precise DNA sequence of an organism depends on its ancestry, initially on its immediate pedigree and ultimately on its extended evolutionary history. Put simply, our evolutionary history is written in our genes, and it is the molecular evolutionist's task to unravel this history, using the modern techniques of genetic engineering and DNA analysis.

In this chapter, I shall be taking a detailed look, from a molecular biologist's viewpoint, at the important contributions that DNA analysis can make to the study of human evolution. Four major questions will be addressed. Firstly, can we use DNA sequence comparisons to establish a phylogeny for recent human evolution and re-create the evolutionary tree linking man with his closest living relatives, the great apes? Secondly, can we use the molecular evidence to date the times of species divergence in recent hominoid evolution? Thirdly, what do these comparisons tell us about the molecular mechanisms which alter or mutate DNA and the evolutionary processes which lead to the establishment of new genetic forms during evolution? Fourthly, can DNA studies reveal anything about the molecular basis of phenotypic (morphological and behavioural) adaptation? I shall review critically the progress in these areas of research, and discuss some possible directions for future work.

The human genome

Advances in gene cloning and DNA sequencing over the last decade have revealed a bewildering wealth of detail about the molecular anatomy of our

genes and chromosomes, and have completely revolutionized our ideas about
the nature of information storage in DNA, the organization of genes, and the
processes of mutation (Lewin 1983). Much of this information is of direct
relevance to understanding the human evolutionary process, and it is therefore necessary to review briefly some of the basic features of our genes before
considering the molecular evidence of human evolution.

The human diploid genome is comprised of 6×10^9 base pairs of DNA
packaged within 23 pairs of chromosomes in the nucleus. This genome arises
from two very similar haploid DNA complements of 3×10^9 base pairs (23
chromosomes) inherited from each parent. The precise DNA sequence of the
genome is unique to an individual. The haploid genome size of man, while
large, is typical for mammals, indicating that what we perceive as the evolutionary sophistication of man is not the result of acquiring extra DNA
information, but instead must arise primarily by the evolutionary modula-
tion of pre-existing genes.

The organization of a typical region of the human genome (or indeed any
other animal's genome) is shown schematically in Fig. 3.1. The basic
informational element in DNA is the gene, a linear sequence of base pairs

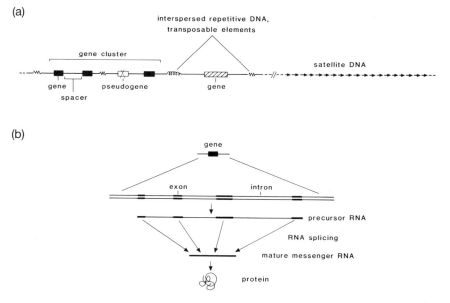

Fig. 3.1.   Organization of the mammalian genome. (*a*) A schematic representation
of typical regions of animal chromosomes. To give some idea of scale, an animal gene
is generally several thousand base pairs long, whereas a typical animal chromosome
contains $c.10^8$ base pairs of DNA. While the DNA is portrayed as being linear, in
reality it is packaged within complex three-dimensional chromatin structures in the
nucleus. (*b*)The split organization and expression of a typical animal gene.

along the DNA double helix, which encodes the structure (amino acid sequence) of a protein. Most human genes, in common with most genes in higher eukaryotes, have a bizarre patchwork structure in which the protein coding sequence is split into several, sometimes many, blocks of coding information or exons separated by enigmatic DNA sequences called introns. The information in the separate exons is assembled into a complete protein code after transcription by RNA splicing. Most introns have no known function, and yet they tend to persist for enormous periods during evolution; for example, the two introns present in human genes encoding haemoglobin are also present in plant globin genes, suggesting that this structure had been established some 1000 million years (Ma) ago, prior to the divergence of animals and plants (see Jeffreys *et al.* 1983). While the significance of introns is not yet fully understood, it is suspected that they may be relics of some very early events in the evolution of genes (Doolittle 1978; Cornish-Bowden 1985). In addition, their persistence in modern eukaryotes has opened up novel avenues for generating complex genes by the rearrangement of exons in pre-existing genes (Gilbert 1978), as well as by the more conventional process of base mutation. The structures of many animal genes bear clear witness to this mechanism of exon amplification and rearrangement leading to ever more complex genes (see Jeffreys and Harris 1982; Maeda *et al.* 1984).

New genes are almost always generated by the duplication of pre-existing genes rather than *de novo* (a statistically highly improbable event) (Ohno 1970). As a result, many human genes form gene families of evolutionarily-related DNA sequences. In some instances, individual members of a gene family have diverged from each other to produce distinct specialized gene products, for example, the haemoglobin gene family (Jeffreys *et al.* 1983). In other cases, such as the genes coding for ribosomal RNA, the gene family consists of many closely related genes each encoding a very similar or identical gene product (see Arnheim 1983).

Gene duplication usually occurs by tandem duplication of a DNA segment including a gene, with the result that members of a gene family tend frequently to be located near each other to form a cluster of genes, with each gene separated from the next by 'spacer' DNA (Fig. 3.1). In most clusters, the spacers are long, and, together with introns in the genes, can account for practically all of the DNA within a cluster. While embedded within spacers there are doubtless regulatory DNA sequences involved in controlling gene expression during development, it is entirely likely that, since there is no obvious advantage to having a small 'streamlined' genome, much of this spacer DNA may be junk, which is of no functional relevance but which has fortuitously accumulated by processes of DNA duplication. By this argument, it is possible that 90 per cent or more of our DNA is junk, punctuated occasionally by functional genes (Ohno 1980).

Clear examples of junk DNA are pseudogenes, DNA sequences which are related to functional genes but which carry various mutations which prevent their expression (see Jeffreys and Harris 1984). Some pseudogenes arise by gene duplication followed by silencing of one of the duplicated genes. These silenced genes persist within the parent gene cluster as 'rotting hulks', gradually being eroded by mutation over many millions of years, until either reduced to a random DNA sequence or lost accidentally by deletion. Other gene relics, termed processed pseudogenes, arise in a more bizarre fashion; messenger RNA molecules from functional genes are apparently converted into a DNA copy and reinserted back into the germ-line genome (Hollis *et al.* 1982; Rogers 1984). For some genes, these apparently non-functional processed pseudogenes can be very numerous; for instance, the human genome contains a single gene coding for the enzyme argininosuccinate synthetase, a urea cycle enzyme, plus at least seven processed pseudogenes derived from this gene and scattered around the human chromosomes (Freytag *et al.* 1984).

The tendency for certain classes of DNA sequence to make additional copies of themselves leads to gene family expansion driven primarily from within the genome by over-replication rather than from without by natural selection at the organismal level (this is so-called 'selfish' DNA; Doolittle and Sapienza 1980; Orgel and Crick 1980). This tendency is amply illustrated by interpersed repetitive DNA sequences, such as the Alu sequence, a short DNA segment present in 300 000 copies dispersed around the human genome (Schmid and Jelinek 1982) and probably originally derived from a processed pseudogene (see Brown 1984). Successive tandem DNA duplications by unequal crossing-over can also lead to the massive duplication of short DNA sequences to produce very long tandem repetitive arrays of 'satellite' DNA (see Dover and Flavell 1982) (Fig. 3.1). Satellite DNA sequences make up a significant proportion of our chromosomal DNA, yet again their function (if any) remains enigmatic.

Finally, not all of our DNA lies within chromosomes in the nucleus. Mitochondria also contain their own DNA as a simple 16 500 base-pair-long, circular molecule present in many copies in each cell and inherited down the maternal side only. Unlike nuclear DNA, the mitochondrial genome is a model of economy, densely packed with a number of genes involved in mitochondrial biogenesis, and with little if any spare or junk DNA (Anderson *et al.* 1981; Brown 1983).

The phylogeny problem

The contemporary hominoids are man, the chimpanzee, gorilla, orang-utan, and the hylobatids (gibbons, siamang). A large number of hypothetical evolutionary trees connecting these hominoids can be constructed, and a few of these are shown in Fig. 3.2. The problem is to determine which phylogeny

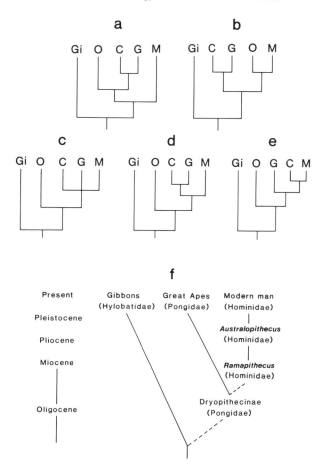

Fig. 3.2. Some of the possible hominoid phylogenies. *M*, man; *C*, chimpanzee, *G*, gorilla; *O*, orang-utan; *Gi*, gibbon. (*a*) is a 'classical' phylogeny, linking the great apes into a single clade. (*b*) shows man and orang-utan closely related, as supported by Schwartz (1984). (*c–e*) are alternative phylogenies with man linked specifically to the African apes, either in a 'big-bang' trichotomy (*c*) or by successive dichotomies (*d, e*). (*f*) shows a 'classical' phylogeny, equivalent to (*a*), relating extant hominoids to fossil ancestors, and is taken from Andrews (1982) with permission. Several independent lines of molecular evidence point to (*e*) being the most likely phylogeny.

is correct and to date the divergence points (each point corresponding genetically to the point of reproductive isolation of an ancestral population). A correctly dated phylogeny is vital for speculations on the characteristics of the earliest hominid, for the interpretation of new hominoid fossil evidence, and for a directed search for early hominid remains.

Classical reconstructions of human phylogeny have depended primarily on the comparative anatomy and behaviour of extant hominoids and on the fossil record (see Tuttle 1975; Simons 1976; Walker 1976; Kluge 1983). A typical evolutionary tree constructed from these traditional approaches is shown in Fig. 3.2*f*; essentially, it groups the great apes together as a clade and postulates an early divergence of this group from the hominid lineage, some 15–20 million years (Ma) ago. This phylogeny is critically dependent on the interpretation of the Miocene genera *Ramapithecus* and *Sivapithecus* as fossil hominids, not hominoids.

More recently, Schwartz (1984) has made a strong case for grouping man with the orang-utan (Fig. 3.2*b*). It is instructive to consider some of his arguments from the point of view of phylogenetic reconstruction. He cites 21 morphological and molecular characteristics which are uniquely shared by these two species and which are absent from chimpanzee, gorilla, and gibbon. These include a range of dental and skeletal characters such as low-cusped cheek-teeth, reproductive characters including lengthy copulation bouts and lack of tumescence on the female genitalia, and several mitochondrial DNA characters. The first problem is that this list of characteristics is not a *random* sample of all available scorable traits, and as such must show bias. Secondly, the morphological characters are likely to be strongly modulated by natural selection, and we cannot, therefore, exclude the possibility that these concordances between man and the orang-utan are the result of parallel or convergent evolution. Finally, we shall see that the few instances of mitochondrial DNA congruence are also without phylogenetic significance. In fact, the molecular evidence consistently negates the linking of man with the orang-utan, and emphasizes the difficulty of cladistic grouping using characters whose rate of evolutionary change or reversal is unknown. Put simply, a character which changes rapidly relative to the time-scale of a phylogeny, or which is subjected to parallel changes by natural selection, cannot be used with confidence for phylogenetic reconstructions.

Phylogenetic evidence from proteins

Protein structure is determined by the DNA sequence of genes. Prior to the new DNA technology, interspecies genetic distances were studied at the protein level, using immunological and electrophoretic methods as well as amino acid sequencing, a laborious technique, to detect protein differences between the hominoids. It soon became clear that the proteins of man and chimpanzee were extraordinarily similar, indicating a level of genetic relatedness normally associated with sibling species (King and Wilson 1975). Comparison of this level of genetic identity with that of other pairs of species whose divergence time was known from the fossil record, suggested a very recent human–chimpanzee divergence time of approximately 5 Ma ago, wholly inconsistent with the 'classical' phylogenies (Sarich and Wilson 1967; Sarich and Cronin 1977; Wilson, Carlson, and White 1977) (Fig. 3.2*f*). Extension of the electrophoretic approach to the other hominoids confirmed the extreme protein similarity of man and the great apes, but failed to distinguish between any of the topologically distinct trees shown in Fig. 3.2*a–e* (Bruce and Ayala 1979). In contrast, amino acid sequence data strongly link man with the African apes (Fig. 3.2*c–e*), and on the basis of a single amino acid substitution in haemoglobin shared by man, chimpanzee, and pygmy chimpanzee, but not by other hominoids, the phylogeny in Fig. 3.2*e* linking man with the chimpanzee is the most likely (Goodman *et al.* 1983). However, as with morphological characters, it is possible that this amino acid change was adaptive and could have been fixed by natural selection independently in the lineages leading to man and chimpanzee respectively. If, on the other hand, this substitution is selectively neutral (Kimura 1983), then the odds of an identical parallel substitution occurring in otherwise identical proteins in these two lineages are low.

Mitochondrial DNA and human evolution

The mitochondrial genome has two useful features which make it especially appealing to students of evolution. Firstly, it is readily amenable to isolation and physical analysis. Secondly, mitochondrial DNA sequences evolve much more rapidly than nuclear DNA, probably due to the lack of efficient DNA repair mechanisms which serve to reduce the mutation rate (see Brown 1983).

Rather than attempt to determine the entire nucleotide sequence of hominoid mitochondrial DNAs, Ferris, Wilson, and Brown (1981) used restriction endonucleases to cut mitochondrial DNA at specific recognition sites (4 or 6 base pairs long) to produce DNA fragments which could be ordered into a physical map of restriction sites along the mitochondrial genome. Interspecific differences in these maps (Fig. 3.3) arise by gain or loss of cleavage sites by mutation of the target sequences. Note that this data set is unbiased in that *all* characters (sites cut by the enzymes tested) are scored. When different hominoid phylogenies were examined to see which tree required the least number of site changes (the minimum mutation or maximum parsimony criterion), the most parsimonious tree was found to link man with the African apes, particularly the chimpanzee (Fig. 3.2*e*). However, numerous parallel or convergent events (parallel gain or loss of identical restriction sites in different lineages) still remained (Fig. 3.3). Given this level of convergence, the best tree is not significantly different from the 'big bang' tree linking man, chimpanzee, and gorilla in a single trichotomy

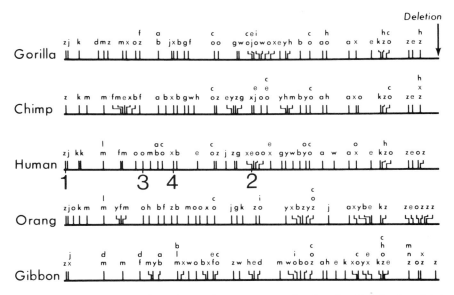

Fig. 3.3. Restriction endonuclease cleavage maps for hominoid mitochondrial DNA. Cleavage site positions are shown for 19 different restriction enzymes (lettered *a–z*) along the 16 500 base-pair-long DNA molecule. The mitochondrial genome is circular but has been 'opened up' at a specific position to facilitate comparisons. Examples of cladistically relevant sites are: *1*, uninformative, present in all species; *2*, informative, links man with chimp; *3*, informative but links man with orang-utan; *4*, informative, links man, chimp, and gorilla together. Such inconsistent groupings indicate parallel evolution occurring within mitochondrial DNA. Figure reproduced from Ferris *et al.* (1981) with permission from the authors.

(Fig. 3.2*c*). Even worse, Templeton (1983) has shown that the level of convergence is highly variable along the mitochondrial genome, and is so great for comparisons with the orang-utan, that the tree is essentially equally parsimonious, no matter where the orang-utan branch is placed relative to man and the African apes; in other words, so much change has occurred in the orang-utan restriction map that no useful phylogenetic information remains.

Brown *et al.* (1982) have directly determined the DNA sequence of an 896 base-pair region from various hominoid mitochondrial DNAs; maximum parsimony analysis now clearly placed the orang-utan and gibbon away from the African apes and man, and weakly tended to link the chimpanzee not with man but with the gorilla. Again, the most parsimonious trees were replete with parallel base substitutions in different branches. Hasegawa and Yano (1984) have re-examined these sequence comparisons using, not the maximum parsimony criterion, but a probabilistic failure model of DNA mutation (Felsenstein 1981). Under this model, the most likely tree is that in

Fig. 3.2*e*, linking man with chimpanzee. Assuming that mitochondrial DNA evolves in a clock-like fashion, the divergence between man and chimpanzee can be estimated at 2.5 $\pm$ 0.4 Ma, an extremely recent and highly improbable date (Hasegawa and Yano 1984).

The above discussion highlights some of the extreme complexities encountered when reconstructing phylogenies even from complete DNA sequence data. The 'best' tree not only depends on the data set examined, but on the biological assumptions and statistical methods used for tree-building. The fundamental problem lies in the mode of mitochondrial DNA change during evolution. Basically, the mitochondrial genome is not uniformly susceptible to change; some nucleotide sites are heavily conserved due to functional constraints, and mutations at these sites are generally eliminated by purifying selection. The precise sequence of other sites is less important and these can accept and fix mutations at a far higher rate. However, the *direction* of mutational change in mitochondrial DNA is not random, but instead shows a strong bias towards transitions (purine $\rightarrow$ purine, pyrimidine $\rightarrow$ pyrimidine) over transversions (purine $\rightleftarrows$ pyrimidine); thus a nucleotide A is far more likely to change to G than to C or T, and a second substitution will equally probably convert G back to A, obscuring the initial change. We are thus faced with the complex situation in which some nucleotide positions are rapidly flicking from one base to another and back in all lineages during evolution, creating phylogenetically meaningless noise, whereas other conserved positions are changing infrequently and are therefore relatively unlikely to undergo parallel changes in different lineages. With sufficient comparative DNA sequence data, it might be possible to identify these slow-changing sites and use them specifically to construct unambiguous phylogenies. To my knowledge, no such analysis has yet been carried out. However, these formidable problems could, in principle, be overcome, not by studying mitochondrial DNA, but instead by analysing a more slowly-evolving DNA sequence in which all nucleotide positions are equally prone to substitution, where substitutions are not fixed by Darwinian selection (which might promote parallelism), and in which multiple substitutions at the same nucleotide site are rare. A possible example of such a sequence is discussed later.

One final word of caution about the use of mitochondrial DNA for reconstructing phylogenies. The mitochondrial genome shows substantial genetic variability within populations, including man, and distinct mitochondrial genotypes can persist in a population for long periods (Avise and Lansman 1983; Johnson *et al.* 1983). At speciation, the two new species may still share a number of distinct ancestral genotypes, although subsequent slow genetic drift will eliminate all bar one in each species. If the remaining genotypes are not the same, then any measure of divergence between the mitochondrial

DNA of the two species will reflect the divergence time of the variant genotypes already present in the ancestral species, and not the time of species
divergence. This consideration, which will only apply to very closely related
species (such as hominoids), may also be relevant for individual nuclear genes
(see page 000); but it is less important for the nuclear genome as a whole,
because here meiotic assortment and recombination of chromosomes very
rapidly scramble any association between specific genetic variants within a
population.

Another curious property of mitochondrial DNA is that it can occasionally penetrate taxonomic barriers. For example, the murine species *Mus
musculus* and *Mus domesticus* meet in a narrow hybrid zone in Denmark, yet
the mitochondrial DNA of *domesticus* has diffused into *musculus* populations over a wide geographical area (Ferris *et al.* 1983). Mitochondrial DNA
exchange and invasion by the occasional interbreeding of closely related
sympatric species is possible, since the mitochondrial genome is unlikely to
contain genes involved in maintaining reproductive isolation or affecting
individual fitness (see Barton and Jones 1983). Put simply, *Mus musculus*
seems to work as well with *domesticus* mitochondrial DNA as with its own.
The frequency during evolution at which interspecific mitochondrial DNA
invasion occurs is not known, but whenever it does occur it will obscure the
true species divergence time assessed by mitochondrial DNA comparisons.

Evolution of hominoid chromosomes

The haploid chromosome set of man consists of 23 chromosomes, compared
with 24 in the chimpanzee, gorilla, and orang-utan. Very detailed karyotypic
maps of human chromosomes, comprised of 1000 distinct chromosomal
bands, have been constructed using high-resolution G-banding of extended
prophase chromosomes. Yunis and Prakash (1982) have carried out a
detailed comparison of this chromosome banding map in man and the great
apes (Fig. 3.4*A*). Remarkably, they can identify all 1000 human bands in each
of the apes, provided that a number of simple evolutionary rearrangements
are postulated (chromosome inversions, translocations and segmental trans-
positions plus fusion of two chimp-like chromosomes in man to reduce the
haploid set from 24 to 23). Clearly, the large-scale organization of chromosomal DNA, reflected in chromosome banding patterns, has remained very
constant in all hominoids, and establishes that rapid phenotypic change in
human evolution has not been accompanied by major reorganization of the
human genome. By looking for pairs of hominoids which share the same
derived chromosomal rearrangement, Yunis and Prakash were able to reconstruct a hominoid phylogeny together with the evolutionary sequence of
chromosome rearrangements and the karyotypes of ancestral hominoids.

(a)

(b)

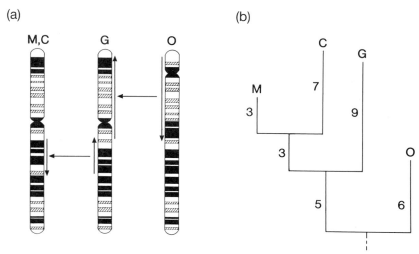

Fig. 3.4. Chromosome phylogeny of the hominoids. (*a*) High-resolution G-banding pattern of a typical chromosome (chromosome 7) from man (*M*), chimpanzee (*C*), gorilla (*G*) and orang-utan (*O*). All four chromosomes can be interconverted by means of two inversions; since the orang-utan pattern is similar to that of rhesus monkey and baboon, it probably represents the ancestral state. The identical chimpanzee and human chromosomes most probably evolved by inversion of a gorilla-like intermediate in the common ancestor of chimpanzee and man. (B) Maximum parsimony hominoid phylogeny (cladogram) derived from analysis of the entire karyotype; branch lengths are proportional to the number of rearrangements (numbered). Data taken from Yunis and Prakash (1982) with permission from the authors.

This maximum parsimony tree (Fig. 3.4*B*), which is apparently devoid of parallel events, again groups man with the African apes and specifically with the chimpanzee. Interestingly, only three chromosome rearrangements have occurred in man subsequent to the emergence of the earliest hominid, which indicates that the gross organization of our genome is very close indeed to that of the last common ancestor of man and chimpanzee.

The hominoid phylogeny deduced from total genome hybridization analysis

The complete DNA sequence of all hominoid nuclear genomes would settle the phylogeny problem once and for all, although, with a haploid genome size of 3×10^9 base pairs, this is hardly a practical experimental proposition. However, the technique of DNA hybridization makes it possible to obtain an estimate of the *average* level of DNA sequence divergence between two species' genomes. Briefly, nuclear DNAs from two different species are denatured to release complementary single strands of DNA, and then

annealed together to reform hybrid molecules, in which the double helix consists of one strand from one species partnered by the complementary strand
from the second species. DNA sequence divergence between the two species
results in imperfectly base-paired hybrids which are relatively amenable to
thermal denaturation, measured by the average decrease in thermal melting
point (ΔT_m) of interspecific hybrids compared with perfectly matched DNA.
The ΔT_m value gives a mean estimate of interspecific DNA divergence
averaged over the entire genome, and for closely related DNA sequences is
approximately proportional to DNA sequence divergence.

   The use of ΔT_m analysis to examine primate phylogeny was pioneered by
Kohne (1970) and Kohne *et al.* (1972). More recently, Sibley and Ahlquist
(1984) have reported an exhaustive analysis of hominoid DNAs using this
method. Their interspecific ΔT_m data (Fig. 3.5*A*) provide some important
quantitative clues about hominoid evolution. Firstly, man and the great apes
have exceedingly similar nuclear DNA seqeuences; even the greatest divergence (ΔT_m = 3.8°C) between man and orang-utan implies an overall DNA
sequence similarity of *c.*96 per cent. Secondly, man and the African apes are

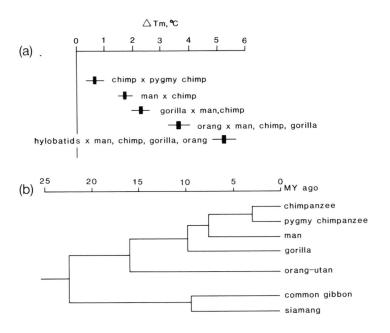

Fig. 3.5. A hominoid phylogeny from DNA hybridization analysis. (A) ΔT_m
values for DNA hybrids between various pairs of species; the standard deviations of
the (many) measurements are given by bars. (b) The deduced hominoid phylogeny,
calibrated using a divergence time of 16 Ma for the orang-utan lineage. Figures
redrawn from Sibley and Ahlquist (1984) with permission from the authors.

most closely related, with man and the chimpanzee significantly showing the highest affinity. Thirdly, divergences show symmetry; that is, within experimental error (which is not negligible in view of the very small ΔT_m values), the genetic distances between an outgroup species A and each of two more closely related species B and C are indistinguishable. This implies that the number of differences accumulated from BCs common ancestor to B is the same as that from the common ancestor to C. This, in turn, strongly suggests that DNA sequence differences are accumulating in an approximately monotonous or clock-like fashion irrespective of lineage.

The ΔT_m data can be used to construct a hominoid phylogeny (Fig. 3.5*B*) in which divergence times can be deduced by calibration of the DNA divergence 'clock' using an appropriate palaeontological reference point (separation of the orang-utan lineage; Pilbeam 1983). The deduced phylogeny probably represents the most accurate picture that we currently have of hominoid evolution, and its full significance will be discussed later. It should be stressed, however, that while the *topology* of the tree is probably correct, the precise divergence times will show uncertainties arising from errors in both ΔT_m measurements and clock calibration, together with possible localized departures from strictly clock-like DNA evolution.

Evolution of genes, gene families and pseudogenes

While hybridization of genomic DNA can provide a detailed phylogenetic picture, it sheds little light on the *processes* of nuclear DNA evolution, and lacks the resolving power necessary for the accurate estimation of genetic distances between very closely related hominoids. Recent advances in gene cloning and rapid DNA sequencing now make it possible to address these questions directly at the nuclear DNA sequence level.

A formidable body of mammalian gene sequence information now exists, but unfortunately this includes very few great ape DNA sequences. Extensive sequence comparisons have been made between homologous genes in different species, and between different members of a gene family in the same species. From such comparisons a number of general rules for DNA evolution have emerged (see Kimura 1983):

1. Functional DNA sequences such as exons in genes usually evolve relatively slowly; this is generally interpreted to mean that most substitutions which change the amino acid sequence of a protein are deleterious and are eliminated by purifying selection.

2. Most substitutions which do accumulate in exons cause synonymous codon changes within the redundant genetic code; such changes do not change protein structure and are preferentially fixed, presumably because they are non-deleterious (selectively neutral).

3. Most of the non-coding regions (introns, flanking DNA) in or near genes evolve relatively rapidly; again, this suggests that lack of functional constraint permits divergence by mutation and neutral drift. Pseudogenes, which have no known function, also seem to evolve rapidly. However, known control sequences such as RNA splicing signals and regulators of transcription tend to be strongly conserved and evolve slowly.

4. Non-coding DNA evolves both by base substitution and by small deletions and duplications of DNA segments. Deletions and insertions of DNA can make the alignment of highly diverged DNA sequences, necessary for estimating divergences, very difficult or even impossible.

5. Substitutions within introns and pseudogenes and at synonymous codon positions accumulate at fairly similar high rates in an apparently clock-like fashion, with a rate estimated at approximately 5×10^{-9} substitutions per nucleotide site per year (see Kimura 1983).

6. After gene duplication, members of a multigene family do not necessarily diverge from each other in this monotonous fashion. Occasionally, DNA sequences may be transferred from one gene to another by a process of genetic recombination termed gene conversion (Slightom *et al.* 1980; Baltimore 1981). After such an event, the two genes will show a region of extreme similarity or identity. Such 'patch homologies' are frequently encountered in gene families, and effectively obscure the true gene duplication time (this is analogous to the phylogenetic problems encountered when mitochondrial DNA penetrates a taxonomic barrier. As a result, gene family phylogenies constructed from DNA sequence comparisons and consisting of a series of dated gene duplications, analogous to species phylogenies in which each split represents a species separation, can be highly inaccurate.

The gene family encoding the various haemoglobin polypeptides has been extensively studied in primates (see Jeffreys *et al.* 1983). In man, this family consists of two unlinked clusters of genes specifying the α- and β-related globin chains. The β-globin gene cluster is comprised of five functional genes expressed at various times during development (Fig. 3.6*A*) plus a single pseudogene termed $\psi\eta$ which also has the exon–intron structure of functional globin genes (Chang and Slightom 1984). This pseudogene contains numerous differences when compared to its functional counterparts; six of these differences would each completely prevent the production of a functional globin polypeptide, and, as such, can be regarded as silencing defects.

The organization of the β-globin gene cluster in the African apes and in an Old World monkey (baboon) is indistinguishable from that of man, establishing that the contemporary organization of the human gene cluster is ancient and was established prior to the separation of the hominoid lineage 20–30 Ma ago (Barrie *et al.* 1981). Thus the stability of higher-primate

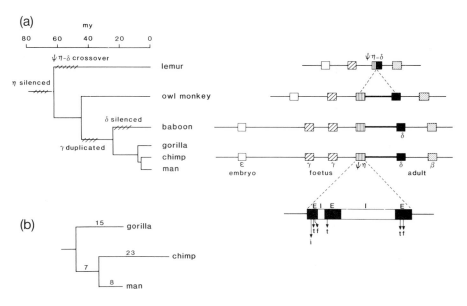

Fig. 3.6. The β-globin gene cluster of primates. (a) The human gene cluster (Fritsch 1980) consists of five functional genes, plus a pseudogene termed ψη which, like other globin genes, is comprised of three exons (*E*) and two introns (*I*), but contains six defects (*i* = defective initiation codon, *t* = termination codon, *f* = frameshift caused by a small deletion or insertion), each of which would inactive the gene (Chang and Slightom 1984). The β-globin gene clusters are also shown for chimpanzee, gorilla, baboon, owl monkey (a New World monkey), and lemur (a prosimian), together with an approximately-dated phylogenetic tree indicating timings of events which have changed gene number and silenced genes; the ancestral primate cluster was probably similar to that of the owl monkey (Barrie *et al.* 1981; Kimura and Takagi 1983; Martin 1983; Harris *et al.* 1984). (b) maximum parsimony tree of man, chimpanzee, and gorilla derived from comparisons of hominoid and owl monkey Ψη pseudogene sequences; the number of substitutions occurring in each lineage over the entire 2200-base-pair pseudogene are indicated (Chang and Slightom 1984; Goodman *et al.* 1984; Harris *et al.* 1984).

chromosome banding patterns is reflected at the much finer level of gene organization. More distant primates (owl monkey, a New World monkey, and the prosimian lemurs) have different organizations arising from gene duplication, unequal crossing-over and changes in the length of spacer DNA (Harris *et al.* 1984). Nevertheless, distinct homologues of the human ε-, γ-, δ- and β-globin genes are present in all primates, and indeed in other mammalian β-globin gene clusters (see Collins and Weissman 1984), which suggests that these distinct versions of globin genes are ancient, and arose by gene duplication before the emergence of the modern orders of placental mammals. Remarkably, this is also true for the human ψη globin pseudogene (Fig. 3.6*A*; Goodman *et al.* 1984; Harris *et al.* 1984).

Recombinational interplay between different globin genes has occurred, for example between the duplicated γ-globin genes (Slightom *et al.* 1980) and between parts of the δ- and β-globin genes (Jeffreys *et al.* 1982), leading to 'patch homologies'. A detailed comparison of gorilla and human γ-globin genes (Scott *et al.* 1984) suggests that these gene conversion events may be fixed quite frequently in evolution and may therefore make a significant contribution to genetic variation and evolution of gene families, in addition to the conventional processes of base mutation (Dover 1982).

Complete DNA sequences of the human $\psi\eta$ globin pseudogene and its homologue in chimpanzee, gorilla, owl monkey, and lemur have now been established (Chang and Slightom 1984; Harris *et al.* 1984). Although from the viewpoint of hominoid phylogeny this list is currently incomplete and omits the Asiatic apes, some interesting conclusions can be drawn.

The six silencing defects in human $\psi\eta$ (Fig. 3.6*A*) are also present in gorilla and chimpanzee, establishing that the $\psi\eta$ sequence in the common ancestor of these three species was also a pseudogene. Extending this comparison to the outgroup species (owl monkey, lemur) suggests that the $\psi\eta$ gene had an early functional history and was silenced very early in primate evolution; it was certainly a pseudogene by the time of the separation of the Old World and New World lineages of monkeys, some 35–50 Ma ago. Subsequent to silencing, many changes have become fixed in the pseudogene, including most of the defects shown in Fig. 3.6*A*. Recent changes in the hominoid pseudogene, which has no known function, are therefore most unlikely to be adaptive, but instead should reflect the rate and mode of neutral evolution driven solely by random mutation and genetic drift. Indeed, analysis of the pattern of divergence of primate $\psi\eta$ sequences shows that substitutions occur apparently at random along the gene, and include both base substitutions and small deletions and additions, as seen for other classes of non-coding DNA (Harris *et al.* 1984).

Of 2200 nucleotide positions examined in the pseudogene, only 51 show variation between man, chimpanzee, and gorilla, again attesting to the extreme genetic similarity of these three species. Using the owl monkey $\psi\eta$ sequence as an outgroup, only 12 of the varying sites proved to be cladistically informative. Three of these informative variants are small deletions or additions; such events are essentially irreversible (the gain or loss of the same few nucleotides at an identical site in separate lineages, when the overall level of DNA divergence is very low, is an exceedingly improbable event) and should provide ideal phylogenetic markers. Interestingly, all three characters specifically link man with the chimpanzee, not with the gorilla. Of the remaining nine variable informative sites which differ by base substitutions, four link man with the chimpanzee, whereas three link man with the gorilla and two link the two African apes. Thus, the most parsimonious tree clearly links man with the chimpanzee (Fig. 3.6*B*) but still includes a small (but highly significant) number of convergent base substitutions. These convergences may be due to specific nucleotide sites which are hypermutable for some biochemical reason, or instead reflect the parallel fixation in different lineages of polymorphic variants which have persisted for long periods in ancestral hominoid populations. The latter possibility cannot be discounted, as the neutral theory of molecular evolution shows that even selectively neutral variants can persist for very long periods (a million years or more for human populations) (Kimura 1983). Such ancestral polymorphisms will contribute a low but irreducible level of 'noise' to phylogenetic reconstructions of closely related species.

Phylogenetic conclusions and implications

All molecular data with sufficient resolving power consistently group man with the African apes and away from the orang-utan and gibbon. Furthermore, studies ranging from karyotyping to DNA hybridization and pseudogene comparisons (together with some interpretations of the mitochondrial DNA data) link man with the chimpanzee. While it would be rash to suggest that the phylogeny problem has finally been solved, it is reasonable to propose that the phylogeny shown in Fig. 3.2*e* is by far the most plausible candidate.

The implications of this phylogeny are clear. Man evolved in Africa, not from some generalized hominoid ancestor, but apparently from a hominoid which shared many of the common features of contemporary African apes. To suggest, for example, that the earliest hominid was partially bipedal, implies that strong convergence towards the numerous morphological correlates of knuckle-walking must have occurred independently in the chimpanzee and gorilla lineages; it is more likely (more parsimonious) to postulate that the earliest hominid was also a knuckle-walker, and that bipedality was a derived characteristic peculiar to hominids.

Both protein and DNA hybridization data suggest that the earliest direct ancestor of man arose very recently, about 7 Ma ago. This indicates that *Ramapithecus* and *Sivapithecus* cannot be fossil hominids, and indeed reinterpretation of the morphological evidence suggests that these genera represent instead early members of the orang-utan lineage (see Lowenstein 1982). The earliest definite hominids are the bipedal australopithecines, dating from approximately 4 Ma ago (Johanson and White 1979); in view of the 7 Ma estimate for the human–chimpanzee divergence, a very rapid early evolutionary shift toward bipedality in the lineage leading to man seems likely.

While this current dating for the emergence of man is likely to be approximately correct, a number of uncertainties remain. First, there are substantial experimental errors in the human–chimpanzee divergence time estimated from DNA hybridizations (Fig. 3.5A). Even if these errors could be eliminated, the dating still relies on DNA changes accumulating in a strictly clock-like fashion. Several lines of evidence suggest that this is not necessarily the case. Firstly, the supposedly constant rate of neutral evolution of functionless DNA, estimated at 5×10^{-9} substitutions per site per year, primarily from human–rodent and human–lagomorph comparisons (Hayashida and Miyata 1983), when applied to the human–chimpanzee pseudo-genes gives a nonsensical divergence time of 1.4 Ma. Preliminary data from various sources now suggest that the DNA clock can show variability in different lineages, and seems to run particularly slowly in primates (Goodman *et al.* 1984; Harris *et al.* 1984). This slow-down is also reflected in a relatively low rate of protein evolution in hominoids (Goodman *et al.* 1983), and may be due to a reduction in the mutation rate caused by an improvement in the fidelity of DNA replication, or due to an increase in generation time. Even worse, there are hints that the rate may be variable even within the primates (Chang and Slightom 1984; Harris *et al.* 1984); for instance, the number of substitutions in the $\psi\eta$ pseudogene are not distributed symmetrically on the man–chimpanzee tree (Fig. 3.6B), but occur preferentially in the lineage leading to chimpanzees (this distortion is significant, $p = 0.01$). Thus the neutral clock seems to have slowed down to the extraordinarily low level of $c.0.6 \times 10^{-9}$ substitutions per site per year during hominid evolution. Interestingly, karyotypic evolution is also slow in this lineage (Fig. 3.4B; Yunis and Prakash 1982). It is remarkable that hominid evolution, which has been accompanied by explosively rapid morphological change, is associated with by far the *lowest* rate of molecular evolution yet found.

These localized rate fluctuations imply that no precise DNA clock exists; instead there seems to be a somewhat erratic clock which, over a sufficiently extended lineage (for example all hominoids, Fig. 3.5B), averages to a reasonably constant overall rate. If the clock does not run precisely, then the dates estimated, particularly for the recent hominoid divergences, can *never* be exact, no matter how sophisticated the molecular data. This is a vital point which urgently requires investigation, ideally by extensive sequence analysis of non-coding DNA from a variety of chromosome locations in hominoids.

There are some interesting taxonomic lessons to be learnt from the evolutionary tree of Fig. 3.5B. First, the grouping of the great apes into the family Pongidae, which excludes man, is phylogenetically meaningless. Furthermore, the extreme genetic propinquity of man, chimpanzee, and gorilla would be much more consistent with their placement, not only in a single family, but in a single genus; this point is clearly illustrated by the congeneric siamang and gibbon, which are genetically *more* distantly related than are man and the chimpanzee. To be consistent, man, chimpanzee, and gorilla would have to be reclassified as *Homo sapiens, Homo troglodytes*, and *Homo gorilla* (which might at least improve our attitude towards our closest relatives!).

Molecular biology and palaeontology—a new fusion?

Molecular biology examines the genes of living organisms and can therefore tell us nothing about the succession of hominid ancestors over the last 7 Ma or so. This situation would be dramatically altered if DNA could be recovered from hominid fossils.

Lowenstein (1981) used immunological methods to search for traces of proteins in hominid remains. Remarkably, human-like proteins have survived in fossil bones of Cro-Magnon, Neanderthal, *Homo erectus*, and *Australopithecus robustus*, as well as *Ramapithecus* and *Sivapithecus*. Significantly, the protein traces from the last two fossils most resemble those of the orang-utan, gorilla, and gibbon, not man, which is consistent with these genera being hominoid rather than hominid (Lowenstein 1982).

Very recently, attempts have been initiated to detect DNA in ancient remains (see Jeffreys 1984). So far, the results are equivocal; DNA has been successfully isolated, cloned, and sequenced from 140-year-old preserved tissue of the quagga, an extinct zebra (Higuchi *et al.* 1984), and from the natron-preserved dermis of a 2400-year-old Egyptian mummy (Pääbo 1985). In contrast, the 40 000-year-old frozen remains of a Siberian mammoth have yielded virtually no mammoth DNA, and what trace is present is severely degraded (see Jeffreys 1984); however, immersion in a peat bog may not be wholly conducive to DNA survival. As yet, there have been no reports of similar studies on hominid fossils, and it is an open question as to whether DNA might have survived.

Molecular studies of human populations

DNA differences exist, not only between species, but also within human populations. This variability is now amenable to direct molecular analysis (Jeffreys 1979; Jeffreys *et al.* 1985; White *et al.* 1985), and in principle it can be used to study the structure of contemporary populations, the phylogeny of human races, and the types of genetic polymorphisms that might have existed in ancient populations of man. Racial phylogenies have been derived from protein data (Cavalli-Sforza and Piazza 1975) and from mitochondrial DNA polymorphisms (Johnson *et al.* 1983); both suggest that there is rather little genetic differentiation between races, at least in part due to the flow of nuclear and mitochondrial DNA between populations by interbreeding. At the fine-structural level of gene clusters, genetic recombination occurs rarely, and, consequently, distinct types (haplotypes) of a gene cluster tend to accumulate (by mutation followed by genetic drift or natural selection) in human populations. It is interesting that mutations causing some of the inherited haemoglobin genetic disorders such as sickle-cell anaemia are often found in only one or two globin gene cluster haplotypes, suggesting that only one or a few mutations (which happened to occur within the associated haplotype) gave rise to the contemporary genetic disease (Kazazian *et al.* 1983). By combining these studies with geographical surveys of the distribution of the defective gene and its associated haplotype, it is even possible to trace the evolutionary source of the mutation and its subsequent spread through populations.

Molecular evolution and adaptation

Man and chimpanzee are extremely closely related and show approximately 98.5 per cent identity in the bulk of their nuclear DNA sequences. While this similarity is impressive, it actually means that the human and chimpanzee genome differ at some 50 000 000 nucleotide positions! In contrast, humans differ one from another at perhaps 5 000 000 sites. In addition, larger scale rearrangements of the genome have also accumulated (Yunis and Prakash 1982; Page *et al.* 1984). These range from localized deletions and duplication of genes and other DNA segments, to insertion of nomadic or transposable elements, transposition of genic segments of DNA, and more gross karyotypic rearrangements. Some of these changes will be adaptive and will be directly responsible for the extensive phenotypic differences between man and chimpanzee. The question is, how many and which changes are of this type?

The bulk of human–chimpanzee DNA differences are probably without phenotypic consequence. Much of our DNA, perhaps 90 per cent or more, seems to consist of pseudogenes and other 'junk' DNA sequences which probably evolve by mutation and random genetic drift without phenotypic effect. A minority of DNA changes will affect protein structure; even here, many changes may still be selectively neutral and phenotypically irrelevant (see Kimura 1983). Thus the adaptive changes driven by natural selection during human evolution may represent a small, possibly very small, proportion of all DNA alterations. It is possible that many of these key differences influence, not protein structure, but regulatory DNA in such a way as to alter the pattern and developmental profile of gene expression, resulting in morphogenetic shifts (King and Wilson 1975). The alternative to this reductionist viewpoint is the holistic idea that vast numbers of substitutions, each with an infinitesimal effect on phenotype, together contribute to altered patterns of morphogenesis; if so, then 'key' genetic changes do not exist.

Simply comparing genes or proteins tells us nothing about the forces, adaptive or neutral, that lead to evolutionary change. Analysis of genes known to have been implicated in adaptive shifts might be more informative. As an example, consider one characteristic of higher primates—the appearance of a distinct prolonged stage of foetal development. The foetus produces its own specialized foetal haemoglobin, which required, early in primate evolution, the elaboration of a specific fetal γ-globin gene. This problem was solved simply by changing the developmental regulation of a pre-existing gene specifying embryonic haemoglobin, without any major revolution either in gene structure or in the organization of the parent gene cluster (Collins and Weissman 1984; Harris *et al.* 1984). However, we know nothing about the changes in the early primate γ-globin gene which were necessary to cause the shift in developmental regulation, and nothing about changes in (currently unknown) additional genes which must interact with and regulate the expression of haemoglobin genes. To give an example of how this problem could perhaps be tackled, consider myoglobin, a protein required for oxygen storage and transport in muscle. Diving mammals such as seals have elevated levels of myoglobin to serve as an oxygen store during a dive. With current DNA technology, it should be possible, not only to determine whether or not enhanced levels of myoglobin result from more efficient transcription of the gene, but also to pinpoint the critical regulatory substitutions (if they exist) by studying the expression of the isolated myoglobin gene after deliberate alteration of the relevant DNA sequences (see Blanchetot *et al.* 1983; Weller *et al.* 1984).

If the reductionist view proves correct, then its application to human evolution will require us to define the types of genes which may be involved in determining relevant anatomical, neurological and behavioural changes. At present, we have no idea what these genes might be, and no idea how to identify them. Unfortunately, man is a very poor experimental system for analysing genetic determinants of morphogenesis. In contrast, the sophisticated molecular genetics of *Drosophila* have recently made it possible to isolate a wide variety of genes controlling, for example, segmentation, determination of developmental pathways, and various aspects of behaviour (see Akam 1984). With luck, the emerging concepts of gene regulation and development derived from this type of analysis will be directly applicable to the study of human development and the molecular basis of adaptation during human evolution.

Conclusion

Evolution is ultimately a genetic process, and any account of human evolution must include the underlying changes occurring in chromosomal DNA. In this chapter, we have journeyed into the strange and complex world of the genome, remote from the familiar fields of anatomy, behaviour, and fossils. We have seen how molecular biology can provide vital clues about phylogeny and dating which complement and extend the conclusions drawn from classical studies of human evolution. We have seen how molecular biology can shed light on the types of molecular process which have altered our genes during evolution. The progress of a field which is barely a decade old is impressive, and the new DNA technology will no doubt play an ever-increasing role in unravelling the history and process of human evolution.

Acknowledgements

I am grateful to Stephen Harris for discussion and criticism. A.J.J. is a Lister Institute Research Fellow.

References

Akam, M. (1984). A molecular theme for homoeotic genes. *BioEssays*, **1**, 78–9.

Anderson, S., *et al.* (1981). Sequence and organization of the human mitochondrial genome. *Nature*, **290**, 457–65.

Andrews, P. (1982). Hominoid evolution. *Nature*, **295**, 185–6.

Arnheim, N. (1983). Concerted evolution of multigene families. In *Evolution of genes and proteins* (ed. M. Nei and R.K. Koehn), pp. 38–61. Sinauer, Sunderland, MA.

Avise, J.C. and Lansman, R.A. (1983). Polymorphism of mitochondrial DNA in populations of higher animals. In *Evolution of genes and proteins* (ed. M. Nei and R.K. Koehn, Sinauer), pp. 147–64. Sinauer, Sunderland, MA.

Baltimore, D. (1981). Gene conversion: some implications for immunoglobulin genes. *Cell*, **24**, 592–4.

Barrie, P.A., Jeffreys, A.J., and Scott, A.F. (1981). Evolution of the β-globin gene cluster in man and the primates. *J. Mol. Biol.*, **149**, 319–36.

Barton, N. and Jones, J.S. (1983). Mitochondrial DNA: new clues about evolution. *Nature*, **306**, 317–18.

Blanchetot, A., Wilson, V., Wood, D., and Jeffreys, A.J. (1983). The seal myoglobin gene: an unusually long globin gene. *Nature*, **301**, 732–4.

Brown, A.L. (1984). On the origin of the Alu family of repeated sequences. *Nature*, **312**, 106.

Brown, W.M. (1983). Evolution of animal mitochondrial DNA. In *Evolution of genes and proteins* (ed. M. Nei and R.K. Koehn), pp. 62–88. Sinauer, Sunderland, MA.

Brown, W.M., Prager, E.M., Wang, A., and Wilson, A.C. (1982). Mitochondrial DNA sequences in primates: tempo and mode of evolution. *J. Mol. Evol.*, **18**, 225–39.

Bruce, E.J. and Ayala, F.J. (1979). Phylogenetic relationships between man and the apes: electrophoretic evidence. *Evolution*, **33**, 1040–56.

Cavalli-Sforza, L.L. and Piazza, A. (1975). Analysis of evolution: evolutionary rates, independence and treeness. *Theor. Pop. Biol.*, **8**, 127–65.

Chang, L.-Y.E. and Slightom, J.L. (1984). Isolation and nucleotide sequence analysis of the β-type globin pseudogene from human, gorilla and chimpanzee. *J. Mol. Biol.* **180**, 767–84.

Collins, F.S. and Weissman, S.M. (1984). The molecular genetics of human hemo-globin. *Progress in nucleic acids research and molecular biology*, **31**, 315–462.

Cornish-Bowden, A. (1985). Are introns structural elements or evolutionary debris. *Nature*, **313**, 434–5.

Doolittle, W.F. (1978). Genes in pieces: were they ever together? *Nature*, **272**, 581–82.

Doolittle, W.F. and Sapienza, C. (1980). Selfish genes, the phenotype paradigm and genome evolution. *Nature*, **284**, 601–3.

Dover, G.A. (1982). Molecular drive—a cohesive mode of species evolution. *Nature*, **299**, 111–17.

Dover, G.A. and Flavell, R.B. (ed.) (1982). *Genome evolution*. Academic Press, London.

Felsenstein, J. (1981). Evolutionary trees from DNA sequences: a maximum likelihood approach. *J. Mol. Evol.*, **17**, 368–76.

Ferris, S.D., Wilson, A.C., and Brown, W.M. (1981). Evolutionary tree for apes and humans based on cleavage maps of mitochondrial DNA. *Proc. Nat. Acad. Sci. USA*, **78**, 2432–36.

Ferris, S.D., Sage, R.D., Huang, C.-M., Nielsen, J.T., Ritte, U., and Wilson, A.C. (1983). Flow of mitochondrial DNA across a species boundary. *Proc. Nat. Acad. Sci. USA*, **80**, 2290–94.

Freytag, S.O., Bock, H.-G.O., Beaudet, A.L., and O'Brien, W.E. (1984). Molecular structures of human argininosuccinate synthetase pseudogenes. *J. Biol. Chem.*, **259**, 3160–66.

Fritsch, E.F., Lawn, R.M., and Maniatis, T. (1980). Molecular cloning and cha-racterization of the human β-like globin gene cluster. *Cell*, **19**, 959–72.

Gilbert, W. (1978). Why genes in pieces? *Nature*, **271**, p. 501.

Goodman, M., Braunitzer, G., Stangl, A., and Schrank, B. (1983). Evidence on human origins from haemoglobins of African apes. *Nature*, **303**, 546–8.

Goodman, M., Koop, B.F., Czelusniak, J., Weiss, M., and Slightom, J.L. (1984). The η-globin gene: its long evolutionary history in the β-globin gene family of mammals. *J. Mol. Biol.*, **180**, 803–23.

Harris, S., Barrie, P.A., Weiss, M.L., and Jeffreys, A.J. (1984). The primate $\psi\beta1$ gene: an ancient β-globin pseudogene. *J. Mol. Biol.*, **180**, 785–801.

Hasegawa, M. and Yano, T. (1984). Phylogeny and classification of Hominoidea as inferred from DNA sequence data. *Proc. Japan. Acad.*, **60**, Ser. B. 389–92.

Hayashida, H. and Miyata, T. (1983). Unusual evolutionary conservation and fre-quent DNA segment exchange in class I genes of the major histocompatibility complex. *Proc. Nat. Acad. Sci. USA*, **80**, 2671–5.

Higuchi, R., Bowman, B., Freiberger, M., Ryder, O.A., and Wilson, A.C. (1984). DNA sequences from the quagga, an extinct member of the horse family. *Nature*, **312**, 282–4.

Hollis, G.F., Heiter, P.A., McBride, O.W., Swan, D., and Leder, P. (1982). Processed genes: a dispersed human immunoglobulin gene bearing evidence of RNA-type processing. *Nature*, **296**, 321–5.

Jeffreys, A.J. (1979). DNA sequence variants in the gγ-, aγ-, δ- and β-globin genes of man. *Cell* **18**, 1–10.

Jeffreys, A.J. (1984). Raising the dead and buried. *Nature*, **312**, p. 198.

Jeffreys, A.J., and Harris, S. (1982). Processes of gene duplication. *Nature*, **296**, 9–10.

Jeffreys, A.J. and Harris, S. (1984). Pseudogenes. *BioEssays*, **1**, 253–8.

Jeffreys, A.J., Barrie, P.A., Harris, S., Fawcett, D.H., Nugent, Z.J., and Boyd, A.C. (1982). Isolation and sequence analysis of a hybrid δ-globin pseudogene from the brown lemur. *J. Mol. Biol.*, **156**, 487–503.

Jeffreys, A.J., Harris, S., Barrie, P.A., Wood, D., Blanchetot, A., and Adams, S.M. (1983). Evolution of gene families: the globin genes. In *Evolution from molecules to men* (ed. D.S. Bendall), pp. 175–95. Cambridge University Press.

Jeffreys, A.J., Wilson, V., and Thein, S.L. (1985). Hypervariable 'minisatellite' regions in human DNA. *Nature*, **314**, 67–73.

Johanson, D.C. and White, T.D. (1979). A systematic assessment of early African hominids. *Science*, **203**, 321–30.

Johnson, M.J., Wallace, D.C., Ferris, S.D., Rattazzi, M.C., and Cavalli-Sforza, L.L. (1983). Radiation of human mitochondrial DNA types analysed by restriction endonuclease cleavage patterns. *J. Mol. Evol.*, **19**, 255–71.

Kazazian, H.H., Chakravarti, A., Orkin, S.H., and Antonarakis, S.E. (1983). DNA polymorphisms in the human β-globin gene cluster. In *Evolution of genes and proteins* (ed. M. Nei and R.K. Koehn), pp. 137–46. Sinauer, Sunderland, MA.

Kimura, A. and Takagi, Y. (1983). A frameshift addition causes silencing of the δ-globin gene in an old world monkey, an anubis *(Papio doguera)*. *Nucl. Acids Res.*, **11**, 2541–50.

Kimura, M. (1983). *The neutral theory of molecular evolution*. Cambridge University Press, Cambridge.

King, M.-C. and Wilson, A.C. (1975). Evolution at two levels. Molecular similarities and biological differences between humans and chimpanzees. *Science*, **188**, 107–16.

Kluge, A.G. (1983). Cladistics and the classification of the great apes. In *New interpretation of ape and human ancestry* (ed. R.L. Ciochon and R.S. Corruccini), pp. 151–77. Plenum Press, New York.

Kohne, D.E. (1970). Evolution of higher-organism DNA. *Q. Rev. Biophys.*, **3**, 327–75.

Kohne, D.E., Chiscon, J.A., and Hoyer, B.H. (1972). Evolution of primate DNA sequences. *J. Hum. Evol.*, **1**, 627–44.

Lewin, B. (1983). *Genes*. John Wiley, New York.

Lowenstein, J.M. (1981). Immunological reactions from fossil material. *Phil. Trans. R. Soc. Lond.*, **B292**, 143–9.

Lowenstein, J.M. (1982). Twelve wise men at the Vatican. *Nature*, **299**, p. 395.

Maeda, N., Yang, F., Barnett, D.R., Bowman, B.H., and Smithies, O. (1984). Duplication within the haptoglobin Hp^2 gene. *Nature*, **309**, 131–5.

Martin, S.L., Vincent, K.A., and Wilson, A.C. (1983). Rise and fall of the delta globin gene. *J. Mol. Biol.*, **164**, 513-28.

Ohno, S. (1970). *Evolution by gene duplication*. Springer-Verlag, Berlin.

Ohno, S. (1980). Gene duplication, junk DNA, intervening sequences and the universal signal for their removal. *Rev. Brasil, Genet. III*, **2**, 99-114.

Orgel, L.E. and Crick, F.H.C. (1980). Selfish DNA: the ultimate parasite. *Nature*, **284**, 604-7.

Pääbo, S. (1985). Molecular cloning of Ancient Egyptian mummy DNA. *Nature*, **314**, 644-5.

Page, D.C., Harper, M.E., Love, J., and Botstein, D. (1984). Occurrence of a transposition from the X-chromosome long arm to the Y-chromosome short arm during human evolution. *Nature*, **311**, 119-23.

Pilbeam, D. (1983). Hominoid evolution and hominid origins. In *Recent advances in the evolution of the primates* (ed. C. Chagas), pp. 43-61. Pontificae Academiae Scientiarum Scripta Varia 50. Vatican, Rome.

Rogers, J.H. (1985). The origin and evolution of retroposons. *Int. Rev. Cytol.*, **93**, 187-279.

Sarich, V.M. and Cronin, J.E. (1977). Generation length and rates of hominoid molecular evolution. *Nature*, **269**, p. 354.

Sarich, V.M. and Wilson, A.C. (1967). Immunological time scale for hominoid evolution. *Science*, **158**, 1200-4.

Schmid, C.W. and Jelinek, W.R. (1982). The Alu family of dispersed repetitive' sequences. *Science*, **216**, 1065-70.

Schwartz, J.H. (1984). The evolutionary relationships of man and orang-utans. *Nature*, **308**, 501-5.

Scott, A.F., *et al.* (1984). The sequence of the gorilla fetal globin genes: evidence for multiple gene conversions in human evolution. *Mol. Biol. Evol.*, **1**, 371-89.

Sibley, C.G. and Ahlquist, J.E. (1984). The phylogeny of the hominoid primates, as indicated by DNA-DNA hybridization. *J. Mol. Evol.*, **20**, 2-15.

Simons, E.L. (1976). The fossil record of primate phylogeny. In *Molecular anthropology, genes and proteins in the evolutionary ascent of the primates* (ed. M. Goodman and R.E. Tashian), pp. 35-62. Plenum Press, New York.

Slightom, J.L., Blechl, A.E., and Smithies, O. (1980). Human fetal g_γ- and a_γ-globin genes: complete nucleotide sequences suggest that DNA can be exchanged between these duplicated genes. *Cell*, **21**, 627-38.

Templeton, A.R. (1983). Phylogenetic inference from restriction endonuclease cleavage site maps with particular reference to the evolution of humans and apes. *Evolution*, **37**, 221-44.

Tuttle, R. (1975). Parallelism, brachiation and hominoid phylogeny. In *Phylogeny of the primates, a multidisciplinary approach* (ed. W.P. Luckett and F.S. Szalay), pp. 447-80. Plenum Press, New York.

Walker, A. (1976). Splitting times among hominoids deduced from the fossil record. In *Molecular anthropology, genes and proteins in the evolutionary ascent of the primates* (ed. M. Goodman and R.E. Tashian), pp. 63-77. Plenum Press, New York.

Weller, P., Jeffreys, A.J., Wilson, V., and Blanchetot, A. (1984). Organisation of the human myoglobin gene. *EMBO J.*, **3**, 439-46.

White, R., *et al.* (1985). Construction of linkage maps with DNA markers for human chromosomes. *Nature*, **313**, 101–5.

Wilson, A.C., Carlson, S.S., and White, T.J. (1977). Biochemical evolution. *Ann. Rev. Biochem.*, **46**, 573–639.

Yunis, J.J. and Prakash, O. (1982). The origin of man: a chromosomal pictorial legacy. *Science*, **215**, 1525–30.

4

Recent fossil finds from East Africa

Richard Leakey

In recent years there has been a significant increase in the tempo of field research into the study of our origins. During the 1960s and early 1970s, research groups were active in Tanzania at the Olduvai Gorge, in Ethiopia in the Omo Valley, and in Kenya at a number of sites of which Koobi Fora is probably the best known. All these localities have yielded fossils of our ancestors which represent the best evidence for the early stages of human evolution. As a consequence of government policy in Ethiopia, and other factors in Tanzania and Kenya, very little fieldwork was undertaken between 1978 and 1981. However, a number of promising sites have been examined in Kenya. During this period, some extremely important new fossil material has been collected and there has been a significant advance in our understanding of certain critical areas.

In this chapter, I shall attempt to review the field as I see it at the present time. This review will necessarily be biased in favour of the East African evidence, with which I have the greatest familiarity, but I see no significant disagreement between the East African and the South African data, and indeed there is no important difference in terms of the later stages of human evolution as documented by fossils from beyond Africa. There are of course many questions that remain unanswered, but today there is a remarkably consistent story for the greater portion of our evolutionary history.

One of the biggest problems that we face in the study of human evolution is the paucity of the fossil material. Many of the current arguments about particular interpretations of human evolution stem from the incompleteness of the fossil record; this has been a problem since the first early humans were recognized late last century in Java, now Indonesia. Although a good number of fossils have been recovered from a number of sites, the specimens are all too often fragmentary and incomplete. The inherent difficulties in interpreting evolution from the fossil record are greatly increased when the fossils are few or poorly preserved. This is why I believe that continued fieldwork is of such importance. There is, for example, an extraordinary potential for the recovery of early hominid remains and associated vertebrate faunas in Ethiopia.

Another major problem that is too often overlooked is that of nomenclature. The definition of a species becomes problematic once the dimension of time is introduced, because species will change with time. The problem is to decide at what stage in the process of change it becomes necessary to designate a new species; and this problem is made more difficult when, as is so often the case, the fossil record of change is incomplete. There are many examples of species in the fossil record which are recognized as distinct because of their isolation in geological time from similar earlier or later forms. With the discovery of new fossils, many of these gaps have been filled, and some so-called species have become less obvious as one pattern of morphology has been seen to merge with another. Of course, there will always be gaps in the fossil record; and for this reason it is appropriate to consider whether our conclusions are based upon the evidence that we have, or upon the mere absence of evidence. There are several good examples of the latter case in the study of human evolution, and these may account, in part, for at least some of the frequent debates and disagreements that have occurred in this field.

There has always been considerable controversy over the origins of our own species, *Homo sapiens*. In the early part of this century it was generally thought that modern humans had developed in Europe. The archaeological investigations and the scant fossil remains then available were in agreement. The Neanderthal and Cro-Magnon finds, together with the superb records of the sophisticated use of stone and bone tools as well as art, offered what seemed to be perfectly clear evidence.

With the introduction of radiometric dating and the recovery of new fossils from sites beyond Europe, however, the story began to look more complex. As the focus of attention shifted from Europe to Africa, the observed range of variation increased, and it was soon obvious that *Homo sapiens* was not so easy to define. Some workers have attempted to resolve the problem by introducing finer gradations; the subspecies level of distinction has been attempted, but with little success. Some authors currently make reference to 'archaic' forms of *Homo sapiens*, but it is not always certain which features are truly archaic. As the record is followed back, the picture is further complicated by what appears to have been a transition from *Homo erectus* to *Homo sapiens*. Certain fossils have been called 'archaic' *sapiens* or 'advanced' *Homo erectus*. An excellent example of this is the fine skull and some post-cranial elements from the South of France: the Arago material from Tautauvel. This find has been regarded by some experts as demonstrating the late survival of *Homo erectus* in Europe, and by others has been cited as proof of the very early development of *Homo sapiens* in Europe! Which of these alternatives is correct?

Perhaps the answer is that both interpretations are correct. There is probably little or nothing that actually distinguishes a late *Homo erectus* from an early *Homo sapiens*, and in fact they may be one and the same species. The distinction indicates only the predisposition of the scientist working with the material and the degree of completeness of the comparative data. We should always ask the question: what is the particular adaptation in a species, that distinguishes it from an allied species from which it may be derived. In the case of *Homo sapiens* and *Homo erectus*, it is doubtful whether any distinctive adaptation can be found. Are we here dealing with different species or is it more likely that one represents a slightly more advanced stage of the same adaptive strategy? There are few differences between the 'archaic' *sapiens* and the 'advanced' *erectus*. I doubt very much whether the retention of *Homo erectus* as a true species in the Linnaean sense can be justified. This is a question of great importance for the future.

A number of fossil specimens that have been assigned to *Homo sapiens* are between 50 000 and 130 000 years old, perhaps slightly older. These fossils have been recovered from sites in Europe, Africa, Asia, and the Far East. Regional variants may or may not be possible to discern, but all the specimens are remarkably similar. The characterization of these early or archaic *Homo sapiens* would take in the Neanderthal morphology; thick-vaulted skulls with prominent brow ridges and other features generally taken as 'primitive'. The archaeological record is very diverse during this period, but to me it suggests a remarkable comparability between widely dispersed populations in terms of technological and cultural skills. Although isolation of populations is always a factor in the short term, there would appear to have been contacts in the longer term. I believe that the world of 100 000 years ago was populated by regionally distinct groups of the same species, just as it has been until very recent times. Little is known about the migratory patterns of these people; but among hunter-gatherers with quite considerable technological competence there was probably considerable movement, with consequent exchange of genetic material between widely separated populations. We were then, as we are now, essentially 'domestic' cultural animals; and this fact would encourage such genetic exchange. The selection of breeding partners from different and distant groups is a factor that cannot be overlooked.

I do not favour the idea that the modern form of our species had a single geographical origin. The fossil evidence from widely separated parts of the world indicates to me that *Homo sapiens* in the modern form arose from populations of the more archaic form wherever it was established; and that, similarly, these archaic forms arose from established populations of so-called *Homo erectus*. There are specific examples that cannot be brushed aside, and I am sure that the apparent 'replacement' of Neanderthal by a more advanced form is more a question of migration than of evolution: the fossil record is not in my opinion adequate to discriminate truly at the level of subspecies.

Another significant obstacle to our understanding of this relatively recent phase is the current difficulty in accurately dating fossils and sites that are

between about 60 000 years and perhaps 250 000 years old. A large part of
the fossil sample for early *Homo sapiens* has never been precisely dated by
radiometric means.

The examination of fossil hominid remains indicates that about 500 000
years ago there existed a form of human different in cranial characters to ourselves. In particular, the specimens have a smaller cranial volume and the
brow ridges are much more protruding, with a much lower forehead and an
angled occipital. These specimens are much more different from modern
humans than they are from the archaic examples of our species referred to
previously. They are generally called *Homo erectus*, and examples are known
from China, Indonesia, perhaps Europe, and both North and South Africa.
Whether this is a true species or rather an earlier example of the adaptation
that subsequently develops features that we consider to be *Homo sapiens*, is a
matter for consideration. I personally believe that it is not appropriate to consider *Homo erectus* as a species in the sense that we use this term in connection with living taxa. I consider it more likely that what we call *Homo erectus*
is in fact an earlier stage in the species known as *sapiens*. It certainly appears
to share the same adaptive features. Perhaps a more realistic approach would
be to use some system of numerical taxonomy. Until such a system is in use,
Homo erectus will continue to be a source of confusion, especially in its later
form.

Homo erectus is represented by fossils that span more than a million years.
The earliest examples come from sites around Lake Turkana in northern
Kenya. One of the oldest examples also happens to be the most complete; a
skeleton of a young boy, found in 1984 and dated at 1.6 million years. This
specimen consists of many parts of the skeleton, as well as the skull and
mandible. It is premature to discuss in detail the morphology, but it is worth
pointing out that the boy was large; the estimated height is 5'4'' at the age of
12 years. It is not unreasonable to project an adult height of more than 6 feet
(or 1.6 metres). There are differences in the detailed morphology of the skeleton when it is compared to modern humans, and it will be interesting to consider these from a functional and adaptive perspective. It will also be possible
to compare the new skeleton with older hominid fossils such as the skeleton
of *Australopithecus afarensis*, and for the first time we shall be able to determine just how 'human' *Homo erectus* really was. Apparently the cranial
morphology of *Homo erectus* changed little, if at all, for a period of about
one million years. This stasis or lack of appreciable change in the morphology
of the skull is well documented by the fossils from Africa and Asia, and it is
interesting to note that the geological record shows similar lack of change. It
may be that a peak was achieved in terms of adaptation and there was no
pressure for further change.

The principal adaptation to be considered is the enlarged and more
complex brain, and in this respect there is a marked difference between

Homo erectus and the australopithecines, of which at least two species are known to have been contemporary with *Homo erectus* until about one million years ago. Could such an adaptation have occurred several times independently? I believe that the fossil evidence is unambiguous on this point, and that the enlarged and more complex brain arose only once, in the lineage embracing both *Homo erectus* and *Homo sapiens*. I am increasingly of the view that all the material currently referred to *Homo erectus* should in fact be placed within the species *sapiens* and be distinguished from our modern form merely as an earlier stage in what seems to have been a single evolving lineage.

The significant question is: where did this lineage first arise? What we need is evidence documenting the earliest stages in the evolution of the adaptation of the enlarged brain. There is, of course, *Homo habilis* material, which is known from several African sites. This taxon pre-dates the early *Homo erectus* fossils by several hundred thousand years. Unfortunately, the *habilis* evidence is not very clear, and there is some confusion as to what exactly constitutes the species. The confusion stems from the inclusion in the taxon of several very fragmentary specimens from Olduvai, the locality which yielded the type specimen. The most important feature of this so-called species is that there is evidence for an enlarged and more complex brain. The best example we have is the cranium from Koobi Fora: KNM-ER 1470, and it is useful to consider this rather than the less complete material. The date for *Homo habilis* is about 2 million years, with some specimens being as recent as 1.9 million years. The point of interest is that the earliest *Homo erectus* are close to 1.7 million years. Does this then represent the first example of the specialization or adaptation of the enlarged brain? I consider that this is indeed the case, and that *Homo habilis* is really the first stage of the species that at a later stage is generally considered to be *erectus*, and, later still, is known as *sapiens*.

I propose that we project *Homo sapiens* as a species that can be traced from the present, back to a little over two million years. At certain points in time, changes occur in the basic morphology, but these are better expressed as stages of change rather than as separate species. I would expect that the most plausible explanation of the evidence is that selection for increased intelligence, the larger and more complex brain, and the use of stone implements, occurred only once. Over time and under pressure from stimuli that we do not yet recognize, the modern form of the species emerged.

It is interesting that in Africa there is fossil evidence for other species of hominid that do not show the enlarged brain and associated morphology. The genus *Australopithecus* is considered to have several extinct species which date from about one million years back to somewhere close to five million years. I believe that there is some evidence to suggest that some of the species within this genus are in fact no more than stages within a single lineage, but there is also strong evidence for the existence of more than one lineage. The validity of the genus will have to be discussed elsewhere, but I should point out that I am not convinced that a generic rank is justified. It might be more helpful to our overall understanding if we were to revert to a more simple concept and treat all hominids (bipedal apes) as species within a single genus *Homo*.

One australopithecine species is quite distinct, and this is the robust form known as *Australopithecus boisei* in East Africa and *Australopithecus robustus* in South Africa. These two species are very alike and are probably one and the same thing, with the difference being related to the geographical distance between the two populations. There may also be a difference in the geological age, but, unfortunately, the South African sample cannot as yet be accurately dated. In either event the morphology is very similar, and the evidence for a particular adaptation is apparent. The species was bipedal, although there is limited evidence upon which to base a thorough analysis of the locomotor details. The most striking feature of the species is the enlargement of the molars and premolars. The anterior dentition is similar to, if perhaps smaller than, that in *sapiens*. The cranial capacity is small, and the skulls were very robust. There was strong sexual dimorphism. The most recent examples of the species have been dated at about one million years, and these are also the most robust forms. The oldest examples are between two and three million years old, and at the present time there is an inadequate record to document the emergence of the species.

A more difficult problem is the interpretation of the small or gracile species of *Australopithecus*. A good number of fossils have been collected and attributed to several species, and the most famous of these is also amongst the earliest: the 'Lucy' partial skeleton that has been called *Australopithecus afarensis*. This specimen has been dated at just over 3 million years and it is similar in age and in morphology to specimens from South Africa that have been called *Australopithecus africanus*. At younger sites, especially in Kenya and Tanzania, there are specimens that are slightly different, although they exhibit the small brain and some other features that are seen in the earlier sample.

The story of these gracile hominids has been further complicated by virtue of the fact that certain specimens have been attributed to *Homo habilis*. Another specimen has been named *Homo ergaster*, and yet all seem to belong to one taxon. There is, in fact, one small-brained hominid skull from Lake Turkana that has not been attributed to any species.

The situation has probably been made more confusing by the historical development of our understanding, where certain interpretations were made which might have been different had there been an opportunity for accurate dating. I believe that there is a single lineage of gracile, small-brained hominids: the Ethiopian *Australopithecus afarensis* as represented by 'Lucy' is an early example; and specimens from Koobi Fora and Olduvai are late examples. It is probable, as others have stated before, that this species, when seen in its earliest form sometime earlier than 3.5 Ma, will be quite similar to the grade of hominid from which both the larger-brained and the larger-toothed species can be derived. At present, there are no fossil specimens that are either complete enough or perhaps early enough to confirm this idea.

The few hominid fossils that are known from sites that are demonstrably earlier than 3.5 Ma are too incomplete for effective analysis. The beautifully preserved footprints and the fossils from Laetoli in Tanzania are perhaps the best evidence. There are odd fragments of cranium that have been dated at 4 or 5 Ma, but these tell us very little, and more material is required. There is no doubt that bipedal gait was established by Laetoli times, and it is of considerable interest to know how much further this adaptation can be traced.

There has been a suggestion that the Hadar fossils, which were referred to collectively as *Australopithecus afarensis*, were the same species as the Laetoli form; but there is well over 500 000 years between the sites, and recent studies have suggested that the Hadar sample may contain more than one species. The one point to emerge clearly from recent work is that, whatever *Australopithecus afarensis* may be, it is not a common ancestor for all the later hominid species. My experience with much more complete fossil material from the Koobi Fora collection indicates that relatively complete specimens, including skulls, are essential if things are to be understood properly. Although the number of individual fossil pieces from the Hadar collection are counted in hundreds, there are in fact very few pieces which are both diagnostic and represented by more than one piece. Mandibles and fragments of maxilla, along with isolated teeth, are simply inadequate for a discriminatory analysis.

The middle Miocene presents a similar set of problems. Data have been obtained from collections taken in China, Pakistan, Hungary, Greece, and eastern Africa; but for the most part, it lacks diagnostic elements such as well-preserved skulls. The mandibular, maxillary, and dental evidence is ambiguous, and it has resulted in a wide range of interpretations all of which are subject to change. At present there seems little evidence for any hominid species earlier than 5.5 Ma. A single, but most interesting, find was made by a Kenyan–Japanese expedition during 1983; but the fragment, a maxilla with five teeth in place, is unlike anything seen before, and its putative date of 8 Ma is uncertain. Other material of approximately this age is known from Pakistan, where the fossil remains are *hominoid* and probably unrelated to the mainstream of human evolution.

The hominoid finds from the middle and early Miocene can be categorized broadly into two groups, one having some features in common with *Pongo* and being principally Asiatic, and the other being African and generally Lower Miocene. The former group has been called the 'Ramamorphs', and it includes two important genera, *Sivapithecus* and *Ramapithecus*. The latter group is known as the 'Dryomorphs', and the Lower Miocene African group, and it includes the genus *Proconsul*. Three species of *Proconsul* are fairly well represented in the fossil record by cranial and postcranial parts.

There has been broad agreement that the *Ramapithecus* morphology is similar to that of *Sivapithecus*, and both are considered to share features that relate to both the living orang-utans and to humans. Recently, the genus *Sivapithecus* has been documented in Lower Miocene African sites, and this raises the possibility that the characteristics of this genus may be 'primitive' rather than derived. It has been suggested elsewhere that there may be a grade represented by several quite similar species. The relationship between the Lower Miocene *Sivapithecus* and *Proconsul* species has yet to be determined with any certainty because of the fragmentary condition of the African *Sivapithecus* fossils.

The *Proconsul* data are much more comprehensive, especially for the smallest of the three species, *P. africanus*. A skull of this animal was collected by my mother, Dr Mary Leakey, in 1948, and other material, including a partial skeleton, was found in 1951. More recently, Dr Alan Walker, working with a team from Kenya's National Museum at Rusinga Island in Kenya, collected the most impressive find so far, a series of five remarkably complete skeletons. This material represents both adult and juvenile individuals. The same expedition recovered associated post-cranial remains of *Proconsul nyanzae*, a larger, chimpanzee-sized ape. The detailed analysis of this extraordinary collection will certainly be of crucial importance to our understanding of the early hominoids from the early Miocene of Africa.

One of the significant gaps in our picture of primate evolution in Africa is the period beyond some 22 million years. The Oligocene primates from the 30 million-year-old deposits in the Fayum of Egypt are the earliest African elements, but there is a great deal to be learned about the intervening 8 million years during which it can be assumed that the *Proconsul* species became established. Few late Oligocene sites are known in eastern Africa, and this time period may prove extremely difficult to fill because of the lack of suitable strata.

I have devoted myself hitherto to the fossil remains. Before concluding, however, it is useful to refer to the archaeological evidence for early human behaviour patterns. There is, of course, a very extensive record of stone implements; and, in many instances, these are associated with bone debris at living sites dating back through to the early Pleistocene and even late Pliocene. The earliest occurrence of stone implements is between 2 and 2.5 million years, from sites in Ethiopia. There are several localities with stone tools at 1.9 Ma, and after this date, stone-tool assemblages are not rare in East African localities. It does, however, seem likely that the evidence is confined to Africa until after 1.5 Ma. One of the most interesting but seldom recalled archaeological traces is of a stone structure at site DK in the lowest strata at Olduvai. This structure has been interpreted by my mother as the site of a windbreak or simple hut, where stones were perhaps used to support a series of branches. There are stones piled unnaturally one upon another in small heaps, and these were found in a roughly circular pattern with a diameter of some 12 feet (3.6 m). In my view, this is certainly a 'man-made' structure and is of quite special significance to our understanding of our ancestors as far back as 1.8 Ma.

The earliest association of stone implements with animal bones cannot necessarily be taken as evidence for hunting, and there is a strong probability that scavenged meat was for a long time the main source of protein. The use of sharp tools was essential if meat-eating was to be a part of the feeding pattern, and it is impossible to determine when hunting became a major activity. There is no doubt in my mind that hunting and the killing of prey need not have required the use of weapons that would be preserved in the archaeological record; wooden clubs, antelope horns, and large stones are the most likely objects to have been used to dispatch animals that may have been run down. The question of when our forebears began to hunt large prey animals will be virtually impossible to answer since the absence of weapons may or may not indicate the potential for this behaviour.

Just as the use of hunting weapons is unanswerable, so there must equally be no answer to the early use of utensils as an adjunct to food collection. Had our two-million-year-old ancestors used skins to wrap and carry seeds, tubers, etc. from one place to another, we would at present be quite unable to know this. The use of gourds or skins to carry water is also quite likely in view of our great dependence upon water in the dry African environment. The implication that early hominids had such 'cultural' artefacts has been considered and some authors regard it as an attempt to humanize or modernize our distant forebears. There is no answer, but I would personally see no reason to exclude such 'culture' from primates that were eating meat and making stone tools.

The use of skin as a means of carrying small objects, as in the case of gourds or skins for water transport, does require a degree of abstract thought which in today's terms is basically human. The ability to make stone tools to a set and regular pattern is also a consequence of abstraction: the maker of the tool has to 'see' the finished tool in the raw material before making the tool. The collection of raw material for making stone tools has to be guided continually by reference to an abstract ideal. There are no grounds for doubting that early hominids were making such mental decisions, and the capacity for abstraction obviously existed. Is it, therefore, improbable that a primate with such a brain could have used it in the manufacture or fabrication of simple carrying utensils? The archaeological record is ambiguous at present and we can only speculate.

In concluding, I would put forward my belief that the 'human' pattern of life, as opposed to the patterns seen in chimpanzees, baboons, or other primates, is distinct and has a long history. The attempts to de-humanize our ancestors are difficult to understand from a purely objective perspective, but it should be noted that there is little fossil evidence that can, conversely, be used to support a more human model either. We do have an excellent fossil record, and the pattern of evolution involving increased brain size goes back to about two million years, and appears to correspond closely with the use of stone for tool-making/meat-eating. Perhaps further field research and analysis will lead to a more complete understanding in future. I believe that the chances are good that we can learn much more.

5

Homo sapiens: single or multiple origin?

C.B. Stringer

Introduction

The origins of the varieties of modern humans have been a source of debate
from before the time of Darwin, but discoveries in the last few years are
beginning to throw a fascinating new light on this problem. Before I discuss
these new discoveries, I ought to explain the way in which I use the term
'modern' human or 'modern' *Homo sapiens*. For the last twenty years
(Campbell 1964) the most widely adopted classification of early hominids has
grouped a number of fossil forms such as Neanderthal man, Steinheim,
Broken Hill, Solo, and 'Mount Carmel Man' as subspecies of our own species
H. sapiens (e.g. as *H. sapiens neanderthalensis, H. sapiens steinheimensis,
H. sapiens rhodesiensis, H. sapiens soloensis*, and *H. sapiens palestinus*,
respectively). In this classification, modern humans are all referred to one
subspecies *H. sapiens sapiens* (although earlier workers had referred the
modern human varieties to different geographical subspecies as well). The
present system of classifying fossil forms as subspecies of *H. sapiens* has
various problems, not least because many workers now refer *H. sapiens
soloensis* to *H. erectus*, and divide *H. sapiens palestinus* into two distinct
groups corresponding with the subspecies *neanderthalensis* and *sapiens*.
Worse still, the subspecies are not defined in a consistent fashion. So in this
chapter, the terms 'modern humans' and '*H. sapiens*' will be used to refer to
the modern human type only, unless it is prefixed by some additional term
such as 'archaic' or 'primitive'.

A brief discussion is also necessary on a point which all too often receives
no attention at all—what are the distinguishing features of (modern) *H.
sapiens*? Some workers assume that everyone knows what anatomical characters constitute the species *H. sapiens*, or that such a definition is arbitrary,
but unless this definition is clearly spelt out there is no way of recognizing
whether a particular fossil is of 'modern' morphology or not. 'Matters of
opinion' are not enough in a field which already has more than its fair share
of disagreements between workers. Here are some of the cranial characters
which I use to recognize *H. sapiens*. Firstly, the cranial vault has a relatively
rounded profile, with each of the midline bones (frontal, parietals, and

occipital) contributing to this distinctive shape; the parietals, in particular, are lengthened and curved. Secondly, the brain is large, and its expansion is reflected in a particularly large height, with high frontal lobes and an expanded upper parietal region, as opposed to the exaggerated length and breadth (in the lower parietal region) of Neanderthal skulls and endocasts. Thirdly, brow ridges are usually divided into a middle portion (sometimes strongly developed) and side portions, but some individuals (especially females) may show no brow development at all. Fourthly, the occipital bone may have a restricted central protruberance rather than the strong torus of *H. erectus* or the central depression found in Neanderthals. Fifthly, the face is small relative to the cranial vault, and (partly associated with the small dentition and jaws) it is retracted under the front of the cranial vault. Sixthly, the face retains a fairly flat form transversely, unlike that of the Neanderthals, and the cheek bones are delicately built, with a depression beneath the orbits (canine fossa). Finally, there is a bony chin on the mandible, and the teeth are relatively small with reduced numbers of cusps on some molars.

Moving away from the cranium, it can be said that the whole skeleton of *H. sapiens* is slenderly constructed (gracile), with less muscularity, and relatively smaller joints and thinner walls to the bones than in other fossil forms of *Homo* (including the Neanderthals). The scapula and pelvis show detailed differences from those of the Neanderthals, but the evolutionary significance of these differences is unclear, since few data are yet available from these areas in early *Homo* skeletons. Putting all these characters of the skull and skeleton together for *H. sapiens*, we can assume that these shared features were present in the last common ancestor of all living humans (unless, less parsimoniously, they evolved in parallel in various areas of the world). Armed with this list of characters, therefore, we can begin to examine the fossil record of the later Pleistocene for evidence of the earliest appearance of this suite of 'modern' features.

The first and last question to consider in the search for our immediate ancestors is whether we are dealing with a single origin or multiple separate origins for modern *H. sapiens*. Was there only one restricted ancestral group, in one area of the world, from which we can all trace descent in the relatively recent geological past, perhaps within the last 150 000 years? Or did modern humans evolve throughout the inhabited world in a process running in parallel, from distinct ancestors of the *H. erectus* or archaic *H. sapiens* grade, a process which might be traced back 500 000 years? Howells (1976) has called these two contrasting views the 'Noah's Ark' model (recent single origin) and the 'Neanderthal phase' or local continuity model (multiple parallel origins). Between these two extremes there are a number of intermediate possibilities involving various amounts of gene flow and hybridization, with extinctions in some areas and continuity in others. From the following discussion of the evidence, it should be possible for us to say which

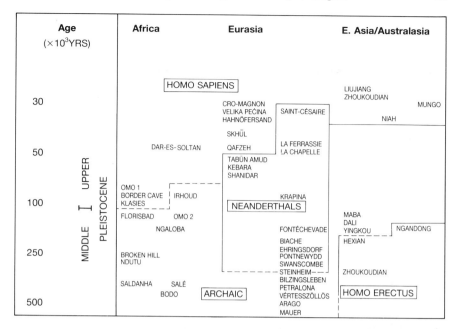

Fig. 5.1. Suggested relative dating of some important Pleistocene fossils, with a possible classification.

of the two extreme models is likely to approximate most closely the actual evolutionary events of the last major phase of human evolution. A source of reference for much of the material and the views discussed here is the recent book edited by Smith and Spencer (1984).

Searching the record beyond 25 000 years ago for well-dated and tolerably complete specimens, matching the character list for *H. sapiens* given above, provides only three areas with unequivocal evidence of modern *H. sapiens*: Europe, Western Asia, and Australia (Fig. 5.1). These areas already show a separation of over 12 000 km, and if we are prepared to allow more fragmentary or less well-dated specimens to be considered, South-east Asia and Africa show evidence of an early *H. sapiens* presence as well. As we shall see, the available evidence points to Africa as showing the earliest records of all. But before considering this, let us review the evidence from the other areas already mentioned, starting with the one which boasts the largest and most informative fossil sample.

Europe

For many years, Europe was considered to be the key area in the story of modern human origins. This was partly because most of the important fossils had been discovered there, and partly because most of the influential workers came from there. More recently, Europe has become an important area in which to test our two competing hypotheses about the origin of *H. sapiens*. Because Europe has a relatively good and well-dated Pleistocene fossil record it is, at present, the best place in which to search for signs of either gradual evolutionary change leading to a modern morphology or a rapid and perhaps intrusive appearance of *H. sapiens*.

Recently there has been a complete reversal of Europe's previous paramount position, as many workers have come to consider the area to be somewhat peripheral to the main events in late Pleistocene human evolution. It is now recognized that Europe probably records a long, gradual establishment of Neanderthal, rather than modern, features during the middle and early-late Pleistocene. While it used to be thought that Neanderthal 'specializations' might be the results of intense selection during the last European ice advance, this model no longer fits the available evidence. Many Neanderthal characters were established long before the last glaciation, and they can be found far from the European glaciers in fossils from Iraq, Israel, and Uzbekistan (close to the Soviet border with Afghanistan). It now seems likely that Neanderthal characters developed over a much longer period of temperate and cold conditions. During the last 500 000 years, European climates have been dominated by harsher conditions than at present. Modern Europeans are fortunate enough to be living in one of the rare interglacial episodes which occur about every 100 000 years, and last for perhaps 10 000–15 000 years. The ancestors of the Neanderthals were less fortunate and had to adapt to the dominant prevailing non-interglacial climates, which even adversely affected the environments of southern Europe. Such probable ancestors can be recognized towards the end of the middle Pleistocene, about 150 000–250 000 years ago, from sites such as Swanscombe (England) and Fontéchevade (France). These fossils were once cornerstones of the Eurocentric 'presapiens' hypothesis of the French workers Boule and Vallois (1957). They were considered to be direct ancestors for *H. sapiens*, quite separate from the more primitive Steinheim Skull from West Germany, which was considered to be an ancestor for the Neanderthals. However, together with material from Biache (France), Pontnewydd (Wales), and Ehringsdorf (East Germany), the Swanscombe and Fontéchevade finds have now been integrated into a model of Neanderthal, rather than modern, origins, which unites them with the Steinheim fossil.

Further back in time, Neanderthal characters become much more difficult to trace as we reach a more primitive stage of human evolution, morphologically and chronologically closer to the earlier species *H. erectus*. Fossils such as those from Petralona (Greece), Arago and Montmaurin (France), Bilzingsleben (East Germany), and Vértesszöllös (Hungary) are probably all older than 300 000 years, and display only scattered or debatable signs of

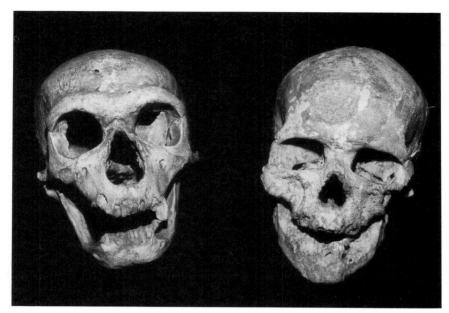

Fig. 5.2. Two of the most significant French fossils compared. The 'old men' of La Chapelle-aux-Saints (a Neanderthal—left) and Cro-Magnon (right). Courtesy of Musée de l'Homme, Paris.

Neanderthal affinities. They may indeed represent very early, barely differentiated ancestors for the Neanderthals, or they may represent a widespread early human species or subspecies ancestral to both the Neanderthals and modern *H. sapiens*. Fossils of similar evolutionary grade are known from Africa and Asia, including those from Bodo (Ethiopia), Salé (Morocco), Ndutu (Tanzania), Broken Hill (Zambia), Saldanha (South Africa), Dali and Maba (China).

Having now established the long history of the Neanderthal lineage and its relatively slow rate of evolutionary change, it is time to turn again to the end of the Neanderthal era in Europe, about 35 000 years ago. As we have seen, the Neanderthals were adapted to the European environments of the last glaciation, and this is reflected in both their body shape and proportions and perhaps also in their distinctive facial structure, with its voluminous and projecting nose (Figs 5.2, 5.3). But the Neanderthals must also have had cultural adaptations to the prevailing conditions, and these are almost entirely represented in the archaeological record by various kinds of flake-tool industries grouped under the terms Middle Palaeolithic (Middle Old Stone Age) or Mousterian (named after the French cave of Le Moustier). These industries also have a long European history, in some cases stretching back into the middle Pleistocene (Cook *et al.* 1982).

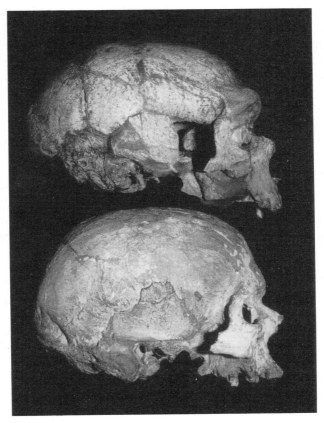

Fig. 5.3. The La Chapelle (top) and Cro-Magnon 1 fossil crania in lateral view. Courtesy of Musée de l'Homme, Paris.

But about 35 000 years ago two new cultural manifestations representing the Upper Palaeolithic appeared in Western Europe. These cultures shared a preponderance of blade tools, systematically struck from cores by the use of a punch. One of these new industries—the Châtelperronian—had clear links with the preceding local Mousterian, suggesting a local origin; but the origins of the other—the Aurignacian—are less easy to trace. The Aurignacian contains greater evidence of the working of bone, antler, and ivory, as well as the earliest indisputable examples of representational art. While some workers still prefer to see the Châtelperronian and Aurignacian as reflecting different local adaptations or activities by essentially the same populations, others believe that they can be attributed to the work of two distinct peoples. It is the latter interpretation which I favour and use here. The appearance of one of these peoples has only become clear in the last few years, following the discovery of an indisputable Neanderthal skull and skeleton in a Châtelperronian level of the Saint-Césaire rock shelter in France (Lévêque and Vandermeersch 1981). In contrast, no Aurignacian site in Europe has produced convincing evidence of anyone but humans of modern type ('Cro-Magnons'). Assuming that the Neanderthal–Châtelperronian and early Cro-Magnon–Aurignacian association holds good in Western Europe, it seems highly probable that the two industries, and thus the two types of hominid were, broadly speaking, coexistent in the area around 31 000–35 000 years ago. There is no sign of the transitional fossils between Neanderthals and Cro-Magnons required by the local-continuity model. After this time there is no further evidence of the Neanderthals, and it is assumed that they became extinct or were genetically absorbed by the early modern populations. However, as some archaeologists believe that the Châtelperronian was in turn ancestral to another Upper Palaeolithic industry, the Perigordian, which was certainly manufactured by people of modern type, there are still problems to be resolved in matching the physical and cultural evidence.

Two French workers, Leroyer and Leroi-Gourhan (1983), have recently attempted to plot the relative positioning of the Châtelperronian and Aurignacian in time and space, and they suggest that there is evidence for a phased and progressive replacement of the Châtelperronian by the Aurignacian, starting in the South of France and working northwards. Could this phased replacement also reflect the gradual replacement of the last Neanderthals in France by the earliest modern people? If so, similar replacement events probably occurred elsewhere in Europe in the period 30 000–40 000 years ago (Stringer *et al.* 1984). The evidence from Central and Eastern Europe is less clear, with suggestions of Middle–Upper Palaeolithic cultural continuity in some areas, but not in others. Upper Palaeolithic techniques may have appeared first in Eastern Europe. The cave of Bacho Kiro in Bulgaria has an early Upper Palaeolithic industry which might be related to the Aurignacian, dated at more than 43 000 radiocarbon years, but the associated fossil hominid material is too fragmentary to identify whether modern humans were also present there at that time. In Yugoslavia there are indications of less 'specialized' Neanderthals from the Vindija Cave, perhaps dating to about 40 000 years ago, and of completely modern humans associated with the Aurignacian at the Velika Pećina Cave, over 34 000 years ago (Smith 1984). Finally, there is a supposed Neanderthal–modern hybrid fossil from Hahnöfersand (West Germany), claimed to date from about 36 000 years ago, and the skeleton of an infant claimed to be of modern type from Starosel'e (Crimea) associated with a Middle Palaeolithic (Mousterian) industry. This complicated picture may resolve itself following further research on the fossils themselves, or it may take the application of new techniques of radiocarbon dating to sort out the contradictory indications of the fossil and archaeological records.

Western Asia

It has long been recognized that fossils from the sites of Shanidar (Iraq) and Tabūn and Amud (Israel) are Neanderthal-like, but it is only recently that research has demonstrated how closely related are the European and Asian Neanderthals (Stringer and Trinkaus 1981; Trinkaus 1983). It has also become apparent that the supposedly 'Neanderthaloid', transitional or hybrid hominid finds from the Skhūl and Qafzeh caves (Israel) are not very closely related to the Neanderthals, but instead have more in common with modern *H. sapiens* (Howells 1976; Stringer and Trinkaus 1981; Vandermeersch 1981; Trinkaus 1984). However, the Asian Neanderthals are not identical to their European relatives. In some respects they are more primitive (particularly the earlier Shanidar sample), in that they lack some European Neanderthal 'specializations', while in other respects they appear progressive (Amud has a small brow ridge—particularly considering that this was a large male individual, while Shanidar 1 has parietal bones of modern shape). But the overall pattern of the whole skeleton of these specimens is unquestionably Neanderthal-like, including details of face shape, skull musculature, and morphology of the scapula and pelvis. As far as can be told, the same is true for the Teshik-Tash Neanderthal child from Uzbekistan.

By contrast, the Skhūl and Qafzeh material shows a preponderance of the characters of modern *H. sapiens* listed earlier, but because there are still features presumably retained from middle Pleistocene ancestors, such as larger teeth and stronger brow ridges, some of these fossils have a primitive or superficially 'Neanderthaloid' appearance. This resemblance does not appear to be an indicator of close relationship, since it is based on primitive features which could be retained from more distant ancestors, rather than on evolutionary novelties developed in common. Thus the region of south-west Asia parallels Europe in the absence of clear morphological intermediates between Neanderthal and modern humans (although we should not forget the occasional progressive features of some Neanderthal fossils, which still need to be explained).

Is there corresponding evidence of cultural change and population replacement in Asia? The answer regarding major cultural changes in South-west Asia is that they occur too late to correlate with a possible replacement of Neanderthals by early modern people. Both the Neanderthals and the earliest moderns of the area are associated with Middle Palaeolithic industries, although the regionally distinct varieties of Mousterian are not particularly similar to those of the European Neanderthals. The transition from Mousterian to Aurignacian or Ahmarian (Upper Palaeolithic) industries probably occurred before 40 000 years ago in Israel and Sinai (Belfer-Cohen and Bar-Yosef 1981), thus providing a minimum date for the Mousterian-associated Skhūl and Qafzeh remains. A figure of about 45 000 years is probably a conservative estimate for the earliest modern *H. sapiens* in this area, since from some data the Qafzeh material could be considerably older than this figure. Accepting a date of 45 000 years for *H. sapiens* in Israel, gives a clear indication of the fact already suggested by the archaeological data. While the interface between Neanderthal and modern humans apparently occurred during the Upper Palaeolithic in France, any corresponding interface in South-west Asia was probably at least 10 000 years older. These data are difficult to explain from a simple local continuity model, since any evolutionary change from Neanderthal to modern in Europe must have occurred later, and under quite different environmental and cultural conditions to those in Asia. However, the discrepancy in dates is readily explained by the phased replacement model, whereby the replacement occurs against a Mousterian background in Asia (*c.* 45 000 years?), perhaps against a Mousterian–Aurignacian background in Eastern Europe (35 000–40 000 years?), and against a Châtelperronian–Aurignacian background in parts of Western Europe (30 000–35 000 years).

The Far East and Australasia

Apart from the extensive Zhoukoudian (Choukoutien) collection, lost during the last war, and the Ngandong (Solo) fossil skulls and tibiae which probably date from the later middle Pleistocene (*c.* 200 000–400 000 years ago), the record of possible immediate ancestors for modern humans is rather poor in the Far East and Australasia. However, there have been important discoveries in China of a well-preserved skull from Dali (Shaanxi Province) and of a skull cap and other fragments from Hexian (Anhui Province). The Dali find is perhaps 150 000 years old, and in some ways it resembles the specimens from Petralona and Broken Hill. The Hexian find dates to about 200 000 years ago, and it more closely resembles the Zhoukoudian and Ngandong crania. A somewhat younger and more fragmentary specimen from Maba (Guandong Province) has been considered to represent the 'Neanderthal grade' in China, while an important discovery of many skeletal parts of a single individual from Yingkou, near the Korean border, should provide much information about the rest of the skeleton in Asian late middle Pleistocene hominids.

It is not at all clear how any of these specimens relate to the ancestry of the modern *H. sapiens* fossils of the area, which date from 10 000–30 000 years ago (Bräuer 1984*a*; Wolpoff *et al.* 1984). These *H. sapiens* specimens include several different individuals from the Upper Cave of Zhoukoudian, and a skull from Liujiang (Kwangxi Province). The former material, also lost during the last war, showed a great deal of variation, but the specimens were quite comparable with their European 'Cro-Magnon' counterparts, and did not particularly resemble earlier or more recent Chinese material. The Liu-jiang skull is more identifiably 'mongoloid', and a plausible explanation for the differences between the Zhoukoudian Upper Cave and Liujiang crania is that the former specimens represent a less racially differentiated or earlier form of modern human, closer to a common ancestor shared with the Cro-Magnons, while the Liujiang fossil is a more developed or later 'proto-Mongoloid' specimen. It is even possible, as suggested previously, that the Zhoukoudian specimens are related to the early modern populations which must have entered North America from Asia during the late Pleistocene—the ancestors of the American Indians.

However, a number of workers prefer to link the middle and upper Pleisto-cene Chinese specimens in a direct evolutionary sequence, and this has been the prevailing view of Chinese palaeoanthropologists, as well as Weidenreich (1947), Coon (1962), and Wolpoff (1980), all of whom view the Asian *H. erectus* fossils as representing probable ancestors for modern Asian *H. sapiens*. In an extensive recent assessment of human evolution in this area, Wolpoff *et al.* (1984) argued that multiregional evolution rather than the 'Noah's Ark' model best accounted for the evolution of *H. sapiens*, both in the Far East and globally. However, they considered that gene flow was an important factor in the spread of certain 'modern' characters, which could be selected for in appropriate circumstances in the recipient population. In particular, they saw eastern Asia itself becoming a centre for subsequent gene flow to Australasia. In fact, therefore, their model combines elements of the local-continuity and Noah's Ark models; in some areas local continuity was more important, while in others gene flow from elsewhere was a more signifi-cant factor in the establishment of modern skeletal characteristics.

Australasia is a fascinating test area for models of the evolution of *H. sapiens*. Discoveries over the last twenty years have radically changed our pic-ture of the evolution of modern *H. sapiens* and the arrival of humans in Australia itself. It used to be considered that Java was occupied by a lingering population of archaic humans until well into the late Pleistocene. But the Ngandong (Solo) material, on which this assessment was based, might well date from the middle Pleistocene; and we have little information yet about the dating of the earliest known modern people in Java, represented by the robust Wadjak fossils. So there is a time gap of unknown duration, perhaps partly filled by the very modern-looking Niah skeleton from Borneo, dated somewhat controversially to about 40 000 radiocarbon years. If this skeleton is correctly dated, then humans every bit as modern as the Cro-Magnons had arrived in South-east Asia even earlier than the Cro-Magnons are known to have existed in Europe. Doubts about the likelihood of such an event have been partly assuaged by the discovery of equally modern remains in southern Australia, dating to 26 000–30 000 years ago from the site of Mungo, part of the ancient Willandra Lakes complex. Archaeological evidence for an even earlier arrival of modern people in Australia is steadily accumulating, but assessing the dated skeletal evidence alone demonstrates a remarkable similarity between the Mungo skeletons and those of the early Cro-Magnons of Europe from sites of about the same age, such as Cro-Magnon (France) and Stetten (West Germany). Such a similarity in the modern characteristics of populations at opposite ends of the inhabited world about 28 000 years ago is difficult to explain from the local continuity model, even allowing for some gene flow.

The proposed local ancestors of these separate, but similar, early modern people in the local continuity model would be the quite distinct late middle Pleistocene inhabitants of the same areas—the early Neanderthals of Europe, and Asian populations such as those represented by the Maba, Dali, and Ngandong fossils. However, in my view the earliest modern specimens of Europe, the Far East and Australasia (i.e. the Cro-Magnon, Zhoukoudian, Niah, and Mungo remains) are much more similar to each other, despite their great geographical separation, than any are similar to their supposed local antecedents. This is best explained by a rapid and fairly recent spread of modern populations from an original ancestral location to each area, rather than a remarkable convergent evolution under radically different conditions in each of the areas considered. Gene flow could also account for such similarities in distant or peripheral human populations, but it would have to be on such a scale and at such a speed as to closely approximate the conditions of the Noah's Ark model, rather than those of local continuity.

There are complications which prevent a wholesale acceptance of the Noah's Ark model for Australasian human evolution. As already mentioned, there is no fossil material which is definitely representative of the first humans to arrive in Australia, probably more than 40 000 years ago. These first colonizers of the continent may or may not have resembled the very modern-looking Mungo skeletons, leaving open the possibility of local evolution from less modern-looking ancestors. Additionally, the Australian fossil record is complicated by the appearance of quite distinct and more robust early humans towards the end of the Pleistocene. Those workers who favour the local continuity model (e.g. Wolpoff *et al.* 1984) see in these skeletons from Kow Swamp, Talgai, Cossack, etc., specific features of resemblance to the Indonesian Ngandong and earlier *H. erectus* material. It can be argued that Australia was colonized by distinct populations, an archaic group of predominantly local origin (the Kow Swamp group) derived from Indonesia, and a more gracile group (e.g. Mungo, Keilor) derived ultimately from Eastern Asia. Recent Australian variation is seen as a result of this dual ancestry, a mixture of local evolution and gene flow or population movement from further afield in Asia. This is an intriguing model, but at the moment it lacks the convincing evidence of a long coexistence of the two lineages in the area, which must have been maintained for at least 20 000 years.

At the moment the Mungo group is most clearly dated as nearest to the initial colonizing event, and there is still the possibility of local evolutionary change under the special conditions of the Australian environment and a vast and underpopulated continent. This could have led to an increase in diversity and robusticity in certain populations, and, coupled with the use of artificial cranial deformation (identified in some of the robust Australian crania), a reappearance of supposedly 'archaic' characteristics. Only a better understanding of the nature of variation in these Pleistocene Australians, together with a proper chronological framework for more of the specimens, will allow a satisfactory resolution of the situation. Whatever the results, Australasia can never again be considered a backwater in the evolution of *H. sapiens*.

Africa

Although the importance of Africa in the earlier stages of human evolution has long been established, until recently it has not usually been given an important role in the evolution of *H. sapiens*. While many workers thought that the Neanderthals or the Mount Carmel (Tabūn–Skhūl) populations were involved in the evolution of modern *H. sapiens*, few considered that African hominids such as 'Rhodesian Man' (from Broken Hill, Zambia) were relevant to later human evolution. They were usually considered to represent late and relict populations, unrelated to modern *H. sapiens*. Claimants for very early modern humans from sites such as Kanjera, Florisbad, Kabua, Cape Flats, and Border Cave were viewed with great scepticism on the grounds that the specimens were either not really morphologically modern, or if so, were not really ancient.

Recently, however, a number of significant discoveries and reassessments of evidence have greatly changed our picture of the role of Africa in the evolution of *H. sapiens* (Bräuer 1984*b*; Rightmire 1984). Firstly, the age of the 'archaic' African hominids such as Broken Hill, Saldanha, and perhaps Florisbad has been pushed back into the middle Pleistocene. This means that Africa is no longer out of step with the fossil record elsewhere, and that there is more time for the local evolution of modern-looking populations. Secondly, old and new claimants for the role of the oldest modern humans in Africa have had their positions strengthened by morphological analyses and relative or absolute dating methods. A number of additional hominid specimens from South Africa, both from Border Cave and from the Klasies River Mouth cave complex, have seemingly established that humans indistinguishable *in the preserved parts* from modern *H. sapiens* were present at the time of the Middle Stone Age over 70 000 years ago, and perhaps as long ago as 120 000 years in some cases. There is always the possibility that other parts

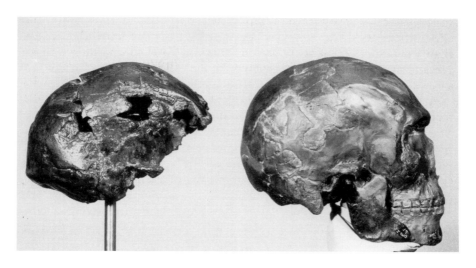

Fig. 5.4. The Ethiopian Omo-Kibish 2 (left) and 1 crania compared in lateral view (casts). The new reconstruction of Omo I was completed by Day and Stringer in 1982, and is shown courtesy of Professor M. H. Day, St Thomas's Hospital Medical School, London.

of the skeleton, or other individuals in the population, were less modern-looking; but on the available evidence it appears that humans at least bordering on the modern skeletal pattern discussed earlier, were living in southern Africa over 60 000 years before their appearance in Europe or the Far East.

Much further north, in Ethiopia, two important discoveries were made by Richard Leakey's team at Omo-Kibish in 1967 (Day 1969). In two different locations partial skulls, one with parts of the skeleton associated, were recovered from sediments containing molluscs dated to about 130 000 years ago. However, the dating method used (Uranium-series) can be unreliable when used on molluscs, so there is some doubt about the accuracy of the determination. Nevertheless, there are radiocarbon dates approaching 40 000 years from much higher up in the section, so the specimens should be considerably older than 40 000 years at least (unless they are intrusive). While the Omo 2 skull has a curious combination of archaic and modern characteristics, the Omo 1 cranium, although more fragmentary, appears much less archaic, and it possesses a gracile and 'modern' skeleton. How modern the Omo 1 skull was, became apparent when a new reconstruction (Fig. 5.4) was made (Day and Stringer 1982). Although the shape of the whole skull must remain uncertain because of the lack of contact between the few fragments of the face and parts of the vault, when tested for the presence of modern features in the better-preserved parts of the mandible, cranium, and skeleton, the evidence was overwhelming that the specimen does indeed represent modern *H. sapiens*. Dated to a time at least contemporary with the Neanderthals of Europe and western Asia, the Omo 1 skeleton provides further supporting evidence for the early evolution of *H. sapiens* in Africa.

North Africa has also produced fossils relevant to the origin of *H. sapiens*, albeit more archaic and less well-dated than some other African specimens. The Djebel Irhoud cave in Morocco has produced two skulls and the mandible of a child, and these have sometimes been incorrectly attributed to the Neanderthal group (Fig. 5.5). They do not, in fact, show any Neanderthal specializations, and instead show combinations of archaic and more modern characteristics reminiscent of specimens such as Florisbad, Omo 2, and Ngaloba (Tanzania). Some dating estimates place them as near contemporaries of the Skhūl and Qafzeh early modern fossils from Israel, in

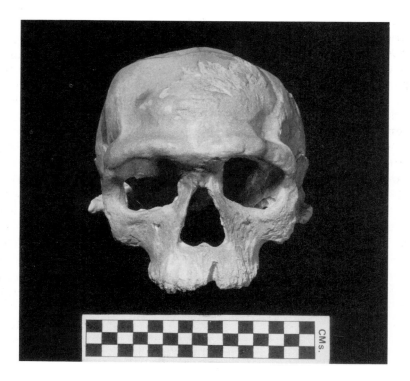

Fig. 5.5. Facial view of a cast of the Moroccan Djebel Irhoud 1 cranium. The two Irhoud crania best represent the hypothesized morphological transition between 'non-modern' and 'modern' humans in Africa, but are uncertainly dated. Photograph taken by British Museum (Natural History) photographic studio.

which case they are probably too late in time to have contributed to the evolution of *H. sapiens* in Africa. However, other estimates date them as perhaps 110 000 years old, and at such an early late Pleistocene date that they could be incorporated into a local African evolutionary sequence leading to the more modern, but morphologically similar, specimens from Dar-es-Soltan, which are perhaps 45 000 years old. The fragmentary mandibular remains from Haua Fteah (Libya) may also relate to the Djebel Irhoud–Dar-es-Soltan late Pleistocene group in North Africa, rather than to the Neanderthals.

Concluding remarks

The African late Pleistocene record, while incomplete and poorly dated compared with that of Europe, contains morphologically transitional fossils which are lacking in Europe between 30 000–40 000 years ago. But any transition between non-modern and modern humans must have been accomplished considerably earlier than 40 000 years ago, at least in sub-Saharan Africa. The transition in North Africa had probably already occurred by 50 000 years ago and, as we have seen, by 45 000 years ago in Israel. Linking the data in rather simplistic fashion, we can put together a staggered 'first appearance' record for *H. sapiens* with minimum ages as follows: Southern Africa 90 000 years (Klasies River Mouth and Border Cave); North-east Africa 50 000 years (Omo 1); North Africa 45 000 years (Dar-es-Soltan); Western Asia 45 000 years (Qafzeh and Skhūl); Eastern Europe 34 000 years (Velika Pećina); Western Europe 30 000 years (Cro-Magnon). Continuing further east we can perhaps include the Zhoukoudian hominids at 20 000 years, Niah at 40 000 years, and more certainly Mungo at 30 000 years.

Unfortunately, we do not have good corresponding dates for the 'last appearance' of more archaic hominids in the same areas, except for the European Neanderthals, who at least were present during the time-span of the Châtelperronian (up to about 31 000 years ago). There is an even younger series of radiocarbon dates for the Amud Neanderthal from Israel, but these dates appear dubious (Stringer and Burleigh 1981). So it is impossible to say how long the hypothesized replacement stage (as the modern human morphology radiated from its assumed original African centre) actually took. Even during the few thousand years of possible coexistence of Neanderthals and modern *H. sapiens*, extensive gene flow could have occurred between the groups. For me at least, there is little indication from the morphological evidence that this happened; but a possible 'bow-wave' acculturation of the Neanderthals at the end of the Mousterian, leading to the production by them of Upper Palaeolithic industries, could be a reflection of cultural contact. This is also a possible explanation for claimed 'modern' features in some archaic hominids (e.g. the Vindija and Amud Neanderthals).

In this brief survey of the evidence for the origins of modern *H. sapiens* I have not yet discussed the evolution of so-called 'racial' features in the fossils. The earliest African *H. sapiens* specimens are not assignable to any particular modern group, although it has been claimed that some of the Border Cave and Klasies fossils are barely distinguishable from their modern sub-Saharan counterparts. If so, this indicates a remarkable stasis in the modern skeletal morphology, once it was established. The Omo and Djebel Irhoud specimens are not assignable to any modern populations, although the Irhoud 1 cranium is reminiscent of both the Dar-es-Soltan and late Pleistocene Afalou and Taforalt specimens, which *are* clearly related to the Cro-Magnons and to more recent circum-Mediterranean populations. The Skhūl and Qafzeh samples may well be close to the ancestral morphotype of all Eurasian modern *H. sapiens*. Within the collection from these sites are specimens resembling in certain respects the earliest modern fossils known from Europe, Eastern Asia and Australasia. Whether they could actually represent an ancestral population for any of the early moderns of Eurasia depends not only on their morphology, but also on the relative dating of the spread of modern humans to the peripheries of the present human range.

The Cro-Magnons of Europe are recognizably similar to modern circum-Mediterranean populations, but differ in a number of respects from recent Europeans, in features such as larger tooth size, larger cranial and endo-cranial size, and body proportions more typical of warm-adapted recent humans (Trinkaus 1981). As already mentioned, the Zhoukoudian crania do not resemble those of recent Mongoloids, but instead more closely resemble Cro-Magnon specimens. They could be related to the ancestry of the American Indians. The Niah cranium from Borneo, the Wadjak crania from Java, and the early Australian specimens from Mungo are not especially similar to modern Australian aboriginal material. 'Local' features seem to appear much more strongly in the later Australian specimens, such as those from Kow Swamp. This is explicable from the 'hybridization' model for Australia favoured by Wolpoff *et al.* (1984), whereby the robust Australian crania contain 'local' characters inherited from earlier Indonesia populations and passed on to present Australian populations, and the Mungo and Keilor specimens represent more gracile populations ultimately derived from those of Eastern Asia, with a different set of 'local' characteristics. However, it is equally possible that in China and Australia the first anatomically modern populations to arrive lacked some of the distinctive features of their modern aboriginal counterparts, and that these have developed since. On this model, local 'racial' characters evolved in the last 50 000 years as modern *H. sapiens* spread across the inhabited world, rather than over a time-span perhaps ten times as long (as suggested in the local continuity model). Thus the evolution of modern *H. sapiens* appears to most closely approximate the conditions of the Noah's Ark model, but it would be unwise to rule out the possibility of gene flow between archaic and modern humans as the modern human morphology established itself globally. Even given the classification of archaic hominids as different species to *H. sapiens*, such species would undoubtedly have been closely related genetically and behaviourally. Finally, the data suggest that the origin of modern *H. sapiens* occurred in two phases. Firstly, the basic suite of modern characteristics shared by all living humans evolved out of a more archaic morphology prior to 45 000 years ago, probably in Africa. Secondly, the features which characterize modern geographical variation were progressively superimposed on the original *H. sapiens* morphology after 50 000 years ago in various parts of the inhabited world. The predictions of this model should be genuinely testable over the next decade.

References

Belfer-Cohen, A. and Bar-Yosef, O. (1981). The Aurignacian at Hayonim Cave. *Paléorient*, **7**, 19–42.

Boule, M. and Vallois, H.V. (1957). *Les hommes fossiles*. (5th edn). Masson, Paris.

Bräuer, G. (1984*a*). The 'Afro-European *sapiens* hypothesis', and hominid evolution in East Asia during the late Middle Pleistocene and Upper Pleistocene. *Cour. Forsch. Inst. Senckenberg*, **69**, 145–65.

Bräuer, G. (1984*b*). A craniological approach to the origin of anatomically modern *H. sapiens* in Africa and implications for the appearance of modern Europeans. In *The origins of modern humans*, (ed. F.H. Smith and F. Spencer), pp. 327–410. Alan Liss, New York.

Campbell, B.G. (1964). Quantitative taxonomy and human evolution. In *Classification and human evolution*, (ed. S.L. Washburn), pp. 50–74. Methuen, London.

Cook, J., Stringer, C.B., Currant, A.P., Schwarcz, H.P., and Wintle, A.G. (1982). A review of the chronology of the European Middle Pleistocene hominid record. *Yrbk Phys. Anthrop.*, **25**, 19–65.

Coon, C.S. (1962). *The origin of races*. Knopf, New York.

Day, M.H. (1969). Early *Homo sapiens* remains from the Omo River region of south-west Ethiopia: Omo human skeletal remains. *Nature*, **222**, 1135–8.

Day, M.H. and Stringer, C.B. (1982). A reconsideration of the Omo Kibish remains and the *erectus–sapiens* transition. *Prétirage 1 er Congr. Int. Paléont. Hum. Nice*, pp. 814–46.

Howells, W.W. (1976). Explaining modern man: evolutionists *versus* migrationists. *J. Hum. Evol.*, **5**, 477–95.

Leroyer, C. and Leroi-Gourhan, A. (1983). Problèmes et chronologie: le castelperronien et l'aurignacien. *Bull. Soc. Préhist. Franc.*, **80**, 41–4.

Lévêque, F. and Vandermeersch, B.V. (1981). Le néandertalien de Saint-Césaire. *Recherche*, **12**, 242–4.

Rightmire, G.P. (1984). *Homo sapiens* in Sub-Saharan Africa. In *The origins of modern humans*, (ed. F.H. Smith and F. Spencer), pp. 295–325. Alan Liss, New York.

Smith, F.H. (1984). Fossil hominids from the Upper Pleistocene of Central Europe and the origin of modern Europeans. In *The origins of modern humans*, (ed. F. Smith and F. Spencer), pp. 137–209. Alan Liss, New York.

Smith, F.H. and Spencer, F. (1984). *The origins of modern humans*. Alan Liss, New York.

Stringer, C.B. and Burleigh, R. (1981). The Neanderthal problem and the prospects for direct dating of Neanderthal remains. *Bull. Br. Mus. Nat. Hist. (Geol.)*, **35**, 225–41.

Stringer, C.B. and Trinkaus, E. (1981). The Shanidar Neanderthal crania. In *Aspects of human evolution*, (ed. C.B. Stringer), pp. 129–65. Taylor and Francis, London.

Stringer, C.B., Hublin, J.J. and Vandermeersch, B.V. (1984). The origin of anatomically modern humans in western Europe. In *The origins of modern humans*, (ed. F.H. Smith and F. Spencer), pp. 51–135. Alan Liss, New York.

Trinkaus, E. (1981). Neanderthal limb proportions and cold adaptations. In *Aspects of human evolution*, (ed. C.B. Stringer), pp. 187–224. Taylor and Francis, London.

Trinkaus, E. (1983). *The Shanidar Neandertals*. Academic Press, New York.

Trinkaus, E. (1984). Western Asia. In *The origins of modern humans*, (ed. F.H. Smith and F. Spencer), pp. 251–93. Alan Liss, New York.

Vandermeersch, B.V. (1981). *Les hommes fossiles de Qafzeh (Israël)*. CNRS, Paris.

Weidenreich, F. (1947). Facts and speculations concerning the origin of *Homo sapiens*. *Am. Anthrop.* **49**, 187–203.

Wolpoff, M.H. (1980). *Paleoanthropology*. Knopf, New York.

Wolpoff, Wu, X.Z., and Thorne, A.G. (1984). Modern *Homo sapiens* origins: a general theory of hominid evolution involving the fossil evidence from East Asia. In *The origins of modern humans*, (ed. F.H. Smith and F. Spencere), pp. 411–83. Alan Liss, New York.

6

Common ancestors and uncommon apes

Adrienne L. Zihlman

The mystery and some early clues

The story of human origins is something like a mystery—one gathers clues from a wide range of sources, analyses them, and finally puts them together to point to the culprit, in this case, the 'missing link'. Where the clues will come from is not always known, and what they mean may not be obvious at first. All of the available clues must be considered before a possible solution to the mystery can be proposed.

Peoples of all cultures express their ideas about human origins and their place in nature in folklore, myths; and oral and written histories. In the Western world, the search for human origins entered the scientific realm with the work of Charles Darwin (1859, 1871) and Thomas Henry Huxley (1863). In his *Evidence as to man's place in Nature*, Huxley discussed the anatomical features which distinguish humans from apes: the structures associated with upright posture and bipedal locomotion, including the pelvis, lower limbs, and feet; small canine teeth; and a brain that is three times the size of a chimpanzee's.

Darwin and Huxley wrote about human evolution when very few fossils were known. Fossil apes called *Dryopithecus* ('oak ape') had been found in France; they are now known to be about 12 million years old. At the other end of the time-scale were fossil hominids, first found in Germany and later in other parts of Europe, originally called Neanderthal and now known to be about 50 000 years old (Reader 1981).

In spite of so few fossils representing a 12 million year time-span, Darwin and Huxley made some interesting deductions about human evolution, that have held true in the light of more recent evidence. On the basis of comparative anatomical studies, they deduced that man was most closely related to the African apes, chimpanzees and gorillas. Therefore they deduced an African origin for the human line.

Attention moved away from Africa during the last part of the 19th and early 20th centuries, when a Dutch military man, Eugene Dubois, sought the missing link between ape and human in the tropics of Indonesia, then the Dutch East Indies. His search turned up 'Java Man', who looked quite human-like but had a brain size about two-thirds that of modern humans.

These fossils are known today as *Homo erectus* and are about 750 000 years old. Their discovery, along with similar finds by Davidson Black in China (Sigmon and Cybulski 1981), seemed to confirm the idea that the human line originated in Asia.

A further misleading clue and another supposed 'missing link' turned up in about 1910 in England, with the naming of the Piltdown fossils as 'Eoanthropus dawsoni'. This discovery seemed to confirm the common assumption at that time that the missing link would have a large brain, an assumption that prevailed until about 1950 when the hoax was uncovered. The ape-like jaw of Piltdown was indeed an ape, an orang-utan, and the cranium belonged to modern man.

A real missing link was uncovered in southern Africa by Raymond Dart in 1925, and was named *Australopithecus africanus* (Dart 1925). The significance of Dart's discovery remained unrecognized for a number of years, dismissed by most anatomists as merely a strange ape found away from the tropical rain forest. Robert Broom, a physician and palaeontologist, joined the search and, during the 1930s and 1940s, he and Dart discovered more South African cave sites and many more fossils (Dart 1948, 1949; Broom and Robinson 1950, 1952).

In order to resolve the controversy that had arisen concerning *Australopithecus*, Wilfrid E. Le Gros Clark, an Oxford anatomist, travelled to South Africa to learn about this strange ape. After careful study he became convinced that *Australopithecus* did have a place in the human family tree (Le Gros Clark 1947). Shortly afterwards, he, Joseph Weiner, and Kenneth Oakley jointly revealed that Piltdown was hoax (Weiner *et al.* 1953). In this way they pruned the ape–human family tree, and allowed *Australopithecus* to emerge as a newly sprouting branch.

By the late 1950s when I began studying anthropology, two pieces of the puzzle were in place. Firstly, based on the comparative anatomy and embryology, the African apes were known to be our most probable closest living relatives. Secondly, the growing fossil record in South Africa confirmed Darwin's original notion that Africa was the place of human origins. Furthermore, all parts of the australopithecine fossil skeleton were now known from the sites at Taung, Sterkfontein, Swartkrans, Kromdraai, and Makapansgat. Although the original skull from Taung was not that of an adult, adult specimens discovered later confirmed that *Australopithecus* had the unmistakable hallmark of 'humanness': it was adapted for an upright bipedal form of locomotion, as indicated by the pelvis, vertebrae, and lower limb bones (Washburn 1951). It also had small canine teeth, as expected, but a small brain. As I began studying *Australopithecus*, I wondered what kind of creature had preceded it.

Clues began to emerge during the 1960s, and to everyone's surprise, they included more than fossils. Now, other kinds of evidence began to have an important bearing on the mystery of human origins. The problem in resolving a mystery, of course, is that all the different lines of evidence must converge to tell the same story, or point to the same culprit.

Australopithecus confirmed and antiquity established

One set of clues from the early 1960s appeared with the work of Mary and Louis Leakey at Olduvai Gorge in Tanzania. The Leakeys began to unearth many important fossils from the Rift Valley—a number of skulls, teeth, and limb bones, from species named '*Zinjanthropus*' and '*Homo habilis*'. These fossils confirmed what was suspected on the basis of the South African finds, that the adaptation for bipedal locomotion occurred in a small-brained hominid, and that brain expansion came later. The presence of at least two species of hominid in East Africa, one gracile and one more robust, lent support to the suspicion that the South African fossils also represented more than one species.

Although the South African caves were rich in fossils, it was difficult to date them accurately. Just how old were they? In contrast, the Leakeys' East African discoveries were susceptible to a new radiometric dating technique—potassium/argon (Glen 1982). A tiny fraction of the potassium abundant in volcanic rock is the radioactive isotope, potassium-40. Potassium-40 decays into calcium and argon with a half-life of 1.3 billion years. When lava flows from a volcano, all the argon gas is vented into the atmosphere, but after the lava solidifies, the new argon produced by the decaying potassium-40 is trapped in the rock. The age of the volcanic rock can thus be estimated by measuring the ratio of remaining potassium-40 to trapped argon.

Luckily for the study of human origins, there has been intense volcanic activity in the East African Rift Valley during the past 15 million years, and hominid fossils found in association with lava flows can now be accurately dated. Before the 1960s the hominid family was thought to have originated less than one million years ago, but the new radiometric dates indicated an age of 1.8 million years for the lava at the base of Bed I, Olduvai Gorge. Not surprisingly, these dates established by the Geochronology Laboratories at the University of California at Berkeley were initially met with disbelief—the time period of human origins had doubled!

Many more fossils excavated from Koobi Fora on the eastern shores of Lake Turkana in northern Kenya, under the direction of Richard Leakey, have added significantly to the understanding of the time period between 1 and 2 million years ago. The Omo River Valley in Ethiopia, part of the Lake Turkana drainage basin, has yielded fossils, mostly teeth, extending back to over 3 million years (Coppens *et al.* 1976). Discoveries in the Hadar region of the Afar Triangle have become widely known because of one fossil hominid named 'Lucy'. Lucy is famous for her completeness, almost 40 per cent of an entire skeleton (Johanson and Edey 1981). This fossil, and many others from the Hadar region, date back to over 3 million years ago. Footprints discovered by Mary Leakey from Laetoli, Tanzania, along with jaws and teeth, push the known record back to over 3.5 million years ago (Ma) (Curtis 1981).

Search for more ancient ancestors

Thus, by the early 1960s, the East African discoveries documented an antiquity for the human lineage of almost 2 million years. This, of course, left unanswered the question: what came before the australopithecines? Unfortunately, then as today, the fossil record is very sparse between 4 and 8 million years ago. In contrast to the late Miocene–Pliocene primate fossil record (4–8 Ma), the middle to late Miocene (10–23 Ma) offers a rich fossil record distributed throughout much of the Old World (Africa, Europe, and Asia), which includes several genera and species of extinct apes and a few monkeys (Andrews 1981). Subsequent specimens have been found in East Africa, Pakistan, and Hungary. Dates of these fossils established by the potassium/argon method indicate an antiquity of about 15 million years in Africa, and about 7 million years for the most recent fossils in Indo-Pakistan (Simons 1981). Among these Middle Miocene forms is the fossil primate *Ramapithecus*, which many palaeoanthropologists believed filled this earliest hominid void.

The genus *Ramapithecus* was named by George E. Lewis in 1934 after the mythical Hindu prince Rama. The few tooth and jaw fragments originally found in India suggested to Lewis (1937) that the genus might be hominid. *Ramapithecus* drifted into obscurity until Elwyn Simons, a palaeontologist then at Yale University, again proposed its hominid status (Simons 1961). The evidence, according to Lewis and Simons, was the supposed parabolic shape of its dental arcade, as reconstructed from jaw fragments. This characteristic shape of hominid jaws contrast with the parallel dental arcade in apes. The upper canines of *Ramapithecus* were said to be too small for an ape. The similar cusp patterns and thick enamel on the molars of *Ramapithecus* and *Australopithecus* were later interpreted as support for the ancestral–descendent relationship of these two species (Simons 1968; Simons and Pilbeam 1972).

Several of Lewis' and Simons' conclusions did not withstand criticism. For example, Eckhardt (1972) pointed out that the dental arcade was not necessarily parabolic. The midline was missing, so that its shape could be reconstructed in several ways. Subsequent discoveries of complete mandibles showed a V-shaped dental arcade, unlike that of living apes or humans

(Pilbeam 1978). Again, thick molar enamel in living species is associated with a diet of hard nuts and seeds that require cracking to extract edible kernels; it is found, for example, in the capuchin monkey (*Cebus*) in South America and the orang-utan (*Pongo*) (Kay 1981). This suggests that dental enamel thickness may have evolved in several different primate lineages at different times. In other words, it represents convergence and is not a good indicator of the phylogenetic relationship.

Molecular clues for a late divergence

While fossils were being recovered from East Africa during the 1960s, and Simons was resurrecting *Ramapithecus* as an early hominid, a number of studies by molecular anthropologists were under way (Goodman 1963; Sarich and Wilson 1967). These critically challenged the supposition that *Ramapithecus* was a hominid; for the evidence indicated that a hominid lineage distinct from the apes could not possibly have been around as early as 15 million years ago.

Molecular anthropologists use the most direct evidence for determining evolutionary relatedness between species—comparisons of their genetic material: the nuclear and mitochondrial DNA. Additional evidence comes from comparisons of RNA, protein amino acid sequences, immunological cross-reactions, and karyotypes and chromosomal banding patterns (e.g. Doolittle 1979; Brown *et al.* 1982; Yunis and Prakash 1982). Comparison of the genetic material and proteins of different species allows one to deduce how long ago they diverged from a common ancestor.

Proteins are made up of various combinations of the basic 20 amino acids, arranged in definite sequences. A given protein may include hundreds or thousands of amino acids. The proteins of closely related species such as horse and donkey are nearly identical, whereas species that separated from a common ancestor more than a hundred million years ago, such as shrew and opossum, have many differences in their amino acid sequences. Sequence differences in DNA and in proteins can be quantified precisely, and their number is approximately proportional to the divergence time (Sarich and Cronin 1976). Such 'molecular clocks' are particularly valuable for evolutionary studies because results can be replicated in different laboratories, in contrast to analyses of fossil bones and teeth which yield subjective interpretations that vary widely from one palaeontologist to the next.

The most startling discovery of molecular anthropology, for those trained in the older palaeontological tradition, is the intimate relatedness of humans and the African apes. Comparisons of blood proteins (albumins, transferrins, haemoglobin) and of DNA itself, have shown about 99 per cent sequence similarity for humans, chimpanzees, and gorillas. Therefore, this triad is as closely related to one another as horse and zebra, grizzly bear and polar bear, or dog and fox. These studies have been extended to dozens of different proteins, and have been tested independently by many researchers. The results are remarkable consistent and support the conclusion that humans, chimpanzees, and gorillas diverged from a common ancestor about 5 Ma ago. This, of course, is in direct conflict with the prevailing interpretation of the fossil record during the 1960s, which held that the hominid line originated more than 15 Ma ago (Zihlman and Lowenstein 1979).

The proponents of an early divergence of hominids from the apes, with *Ramapithecus* as an early human ancestor, could not dispute the data showing 99 per cent identity of the genetic material of man and the African apes. Instead, some of them maintained that primate DNA and proteins evolve at only about one-third of the average rate demonstrated for other mammalian lineages, such as bats, horses, cows, whales, carnivores, and even such non-mammalian groups as frogs (Wilson *et al.* 1977). The conflict between the traditionalists and the new breed of molecular evolutionists has given rise to an enormous literature on the 'molecular clock' controversy. The morphologists who study teeth and bones have generally maintained that molecular clocks do not keep good time and are not valid indicators of evolutionary relationships (Simons 1981; Schwartz 1984).

The picture of evolutionary processes in the genome of eukaryotes (organisms with nucleated cells) has changed rapidly in the past few years (Lowenstein and Zihlman 1984). Firstly, we know now that different proteins evolve at different rates, like hour, minute, and second hands on a clock. Thus, cytochrome *C* is slow, haemoglobin moderate, and fibrinopeptides fast; but the really important point is that the results of different protein comparisons are concordant with each other. Secondly, and contrary to what most of us have been taught, a considerable portion of mutations in the genetic material (DNA), turn out to be neither deleterious nor favourable, and are described as selectively 'neutral'. It appears that many amino acid substitutions do not significantly alter protein function. The more rapidly evolving proteins, such as fibrinopeptides, can tolerate more such substitutions than can the slower evolving molecules such as cytochrome *C* or histone. Thirdly, it seems that only about 1 per cent of the genome actually codes for proteins. Changes in bases of the remaining 99 per cent, sometimes called 'selfish' or 'parasitic' DNA, are four or five times more common than changes in the DNA that codes for proteins (Jukes 1980).

A good scientific hypothesis makes predictions which can be verified or falsified by subsequent observation. The 'molecular clock', as applied to human evolution, predicted that the oldest hominid fossils would resemble chimpanzees or gorillas and be no more than five million years old. As noted, the oldest undisputed hominid fossils to-date, of the genus *Australopithecus*, are dated by the potassium/argon method as between 3 and 3.5 million years old.

What kind of common ancestor?

If humans, chimpanzees, and gorillas diverged from a common ancestor some 5 Ma ago, what was that common ancestor like? There are no visible candidates in the fossil record because there are few primate fossils for the critical period from 4–8 Ma ago. Here, one good fossil would be better than volumes of theories. But rather than accept the tenet that 'we can't know' about this period of human origins, I believe that a combination of clues—molecular, anatomical, behavioural, and palaeontological—may be woven together to provide a plausible picture of that African progenitor.

Firstly, we might ask what kind of creature would have been most likely to give rise to three lines of descent as diverse as the human, chimpanzee, and gorilla. Which of the three, or what mixture of the three, would provide the best starting point? Is it possible that one has changed less morphologically

Fig. 6.1.   Pygmy chimpanzee, *Pan paniscus*, Kanzi, 4½ year-old male. Photograph by Elizabeth Rupert.

during the past 5 million years, and so represents a better model of the common ancestor?

The earliest undisputed hominids, members of the genus *Australopithecus*, living between 2 and 3.5 Ma ago, greatly strengthened the idea that the living great apes and *Homo sapiens* shared a common ancestor (e.g. Washburn 1951). Molecular relationships have now reaffirmed the closeness of humans to the African apes, and they help to narrow the choices for an African hominoid common ancestor. But there has been little discussion, and even less agreement, on what kind of ape was ancestral to the hominid line: How large was it? What were the details of its anatomy and its locomotor pattern? Was it a knuckle-walker? How sexually dimorphic was it?

A chimpanzee-like prototype derives logically from both molecular and anatomical similarities. Though the gorilla is also close to humans genetically, the chimpanzee is more similar anatomically to the earliest known African hominids. The chimp is more 'generalized' than the gorilla; it is

Fig. 6.2. Common chimpanzee, *Pan troglodytes*, Austin, 4½ year-old male. Photograph by Elizabeth Rupert.

smaller, less sexually dimorphic, and more omnivorous; it is at home in the trees and on the ground, lives in a greater variety of habitats, is more social, and uses tools in its natural habitat. Studies on free-ranging chimpanzees begun in the 1960s, revealed unexpected similarities with humans: chimpanzees make and use tools in many ways and from a variety of materials; they also share food, eat meat, have close mother–infant ties, form enduring social bonds, possess flexible social organization, and communicate via complex gestures and vocalizations. Such a range of 'human-like' behaviours not

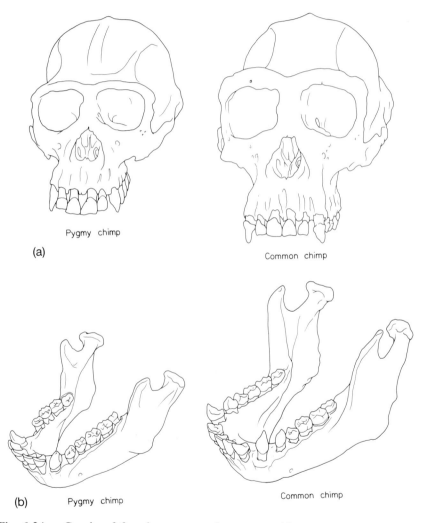

Fig. 6.3A. Crania of female pygmy and common chimpanzees of similar body weights. Drawn to same scale. **B.** Mandibles of female pygmy and common chimpanzees of similar body weights. Drawn to same scale.

only emphasizes how close the two species are, but also serves to aid in the reconstruction of early hominid behaviour (Goodall and Hamburg 1975; Zihlman 1983).

Of the African apes, then, we can narrow the model to chimpanzees. But there are two species of chimpanzees alive in Africa today: the common species, *Pan troglodytes*, found in West and Central Africa; and a rarer species, the pygmy chimpanzee, *Pan paniscus*, confined to a small enclave in the Zaïre River Basin. (See Figs. 6.1 and 6.2).

The two species are equally genetically related to humans, that is, the two chimpanzees are more closely related to each other than either is to humans, and diverged from each other between 2 and 3 Ma ago. However, of the two,

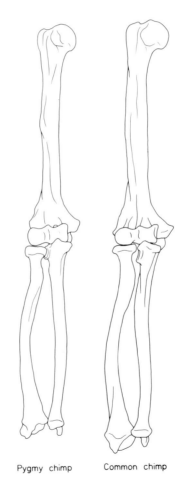

Pygmy chimp   Common chimp

Fig. 6.4. Upper limbs (humerus, radius, and ulna) of female pygmy and common chimpanzees of similar body weights. Drawn to same scale.

pygmy chimpanzees, or bonobos, may serve as a better model for under-standing the morphological precursor of humans, gorillas, and chimpanzees (Zihlman *et al.* 1978).

Pygmy chimpanzees were first distinguished and named on the basis of their smaller skulls and dentition by E. Schwarz in 1929. (See Fig. 6.3A and B). However, their limb bones are by no means 'pygmy' when compared with those of the common species. (See Figs. 6.4 and 6.5). Harold Coolidge (1933) maintained that *Pan paniscus* is a separate, more generalized species than the common chimpanzee, and that it might 'approach more closely to the common ancestor of chimpanzees and man than does any . . . (other) . . . living chimpanzee' (p. 56). Vincent Sarich (1967), integrating the molecular

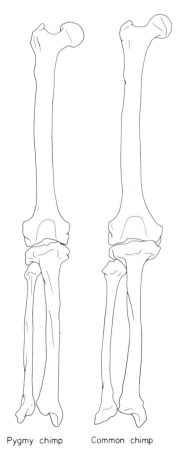

Pygmy chimp   Common chimp

Fig. 6.5. Lower limbs (femur, tibia, and fibula) of female pygmy and common chimpanzees of similar body weights. Drawn to same scale.

with the fossil evidence, also concluded that the common ancestor must resemble a small chimpanzee, like *Pan paniscus*.

Several related questions about pygmy chimpanzees bear on their use as a model for understanding human origins. Firstly, how do the two species of chimp compare morphologically? Is one more 'generalized' than the other? Secondly, do their differences bear on their respective locomotor patterns and, if so, how? Thirdly, how do pygmy chimpanzees contribute to our understanding of the transition from quadrupedal to bipedal locomotion?

Morphological comparisons

On the basis of a single adult skeleton of *Pan paniscus* compared with Adolph Schultz's *Pan troglodytes* sample, Coolidge (1933) noted that the pygmy chimp possessed shorter upper limbs and a narrower chest. My own studies of a larger sample of *Pan paniscus* skeletons confirmed and elaborated Coolidge's initial findings: pygmy chimpanzees are significantly smaller in their chest (scapular and clavicular measurements) and pelvic breadths, but they have longer lower limbs, as expressed in the humerus/femur ratio (Zihlman and Cramer 1978). (See Figs. 6.6 and 6.7.) These differences in linear skeletal dimensions have been elaborated by other studies (Shea 1981; Coolidge and Shea 1982; Jungers and Susman 1984).

Whether pygmy chimps are merely a smaller version of common chimpanzees—in morphologists' jargon, whether the differences are 'allometric'—has been a point of much debate. The skull of *Pan paniscus* is

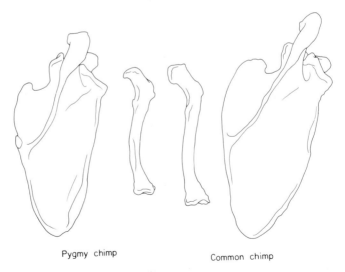

Pygmy chimp   Common chimp

Fig. 6.6. Shoulder girdles (clavicle, scapula) of female pygmy and common chimpanzees of similar body weights. Drawn to same scale.

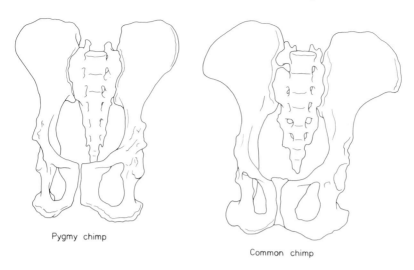

Pygmy chimp

Common chimp

Fig. 6.7. Pelvis of female pygmy and common chimpanzees of similar body weights. Drawn to same scale.

notably more gracile and smaller (which is why Coolidge misleadingly called it 'pygmy'), and the two chimp species can be discriminated on the basis of mandibular length (Cramer 1977). However, it is difficult to distinguish the two species definitively on the basis of skeletal dimensions alone. Recognizing the possible scaling differences, Zihlman and Cramer (1978) compared the pygmy chimp sample with female common chimps, in a number of skeletal dimensions, in order to minimize the differences due merely to body weight.

To measure more accurately the possible differences between the two kinds of chimps, I compared an individual of each species (with similar body weight) using a methodology developed by Grand (1977). This method looks at the whole animal, including skeletal dimensions, and gives information on other anatomical parts. With similar body weights the role of 'allometry' is eliminated, and differences emerge more clearly. Results on two females of comparable body weight, one of each species, showed that pygmy chimps have a 'lighter' trunk (60 per cent of total body weight vs. 66 per cent for the common chimp), and heavier lower limbs (25 per cent of total body weight vs. 18 per cent for the common chimp), but that the two species have similar relative weights in their upper limbs (16 per cent) (Zihlman 1984). These findings further clarify the meaning of the skeletal dimensions in pygmy chimpanzees: the shorter clavicle, smaller scapula, and narrower ilium all indicate a more gracile trunk than the common species; and the longer femur and tibia testify to the heavier lower limbs.

With regard to sexual dimorphism (morphological differences between males and females of a species) pygmy chimpanzees show a unique configuration of features. Body weight differences between the sexes may be marked; a variety of estimates indicate that the average weight for females is 31–33 kg, while that for males is 38–45 kg (see Jungers and Susman 1984; Zihlman 1984). Minimally then, females are 73 per cent of male body weights, or males, 137 per cent of females. In contrast, cranial capacity in the two sexes shows no significant difference. In a sample of 60 *Pan paniscus* skulls, D.L. Cramer (1977) obtained a female average of 348.5 cm³ and a male average of 351.2 cm³, whereas comparable figures for the common chimp are female, 375 cm³, and male, 404 cm³. In dentition there is some dimorphism in the maxillary and mandibular canines of pygmy chimps, but little in the incisors or posterior teeth; in contrast, almost every permanent tooth is significantly larger on average in male than in female common chimps (Kinzey 1984).

Similarly, little sexual dimorphism has been observed in long-bone lengths and joint size in a sample of 20 pygmy chimp skeletons, even though body weight differences are marked (Cramer and Zihlman 1978). In common chimpanzees and humans there is a similar degree of sexual dimorphism in body weight, but there are also sex differences in long-bone lengths, joint sizes and cranial capacities (Cramer 1977; Zihlman 1976; Zihlman and Cramer 1978).

Thus, despite a great deal of overlap between the two chimpanzee species in body weight, cranial capacity, and skeletal dimensions, there are significant differences in body build and the pattern of male–female dimorphism. Pygmy chimps are not simply a smaller version of the common species, and their proportions cannot be said to be allometric.

Whether pygmy chimpanzees are more 'generalized' than the common species must be argued on the basis of particular features. Body proportions of pygmy chimps—relatively longer lower legs to trunk height—may represent a generalized character (Shea 1981). The cranial base indicates that the basicranial lines of *Pan paniscus* are similar to those of the juvenile and sub-adult members of other pongids, and so approximate a generalized condition (Laitman and Heimbuch 1984). It appears then that of the four African hominoid species, pygmy chimpanzees have undergone the least amount of morphological change in some cranial and postcranial features.

Locomotor behaviour

Functionally, what is the significance of the difference between pygmy chimps and common chimps in body proportions, and especially in the distribution of body weight? Both species of chimpanzees have a similar range of locomotor behaviours—climbing and hanging in trees, quadrupedal knuckle-walking on the ground and bipedality (Goodall 1968; Susman *et al.* 1980). From the earliest reports, pygmy chimps have been described as readily bipedal (Tratz and Heck 1954). A locomotor study carried out on both chimp species in captivity confirms that the pygmy chimp uses its hind limbs more actively in climbing and standing, and tends to be bipedal in a greater variety of contexts than common chimpanzees (Zihlman 1980).

Findings based on captive animals have been confirmed recently by observations on wild pygmy chimpanzees at Wamba. In an ethological study by Mori (1984), behaviours were classified into 47 patterns which were easy to distinguish from a distance. 'Bipedal' was the third most common behaviour (268), following 'run' (462) and 'drag branch' (363), and preceding 'present' (139) and 'flight' (138). The reason for the high frequency is that a number of behavioural sequences start from a bipedal posture and then lead into sexual or dominance–subordinance interactions. Such an emphasis on bipedal behaviour (also included in the 'run' category) correlates with pygmy chimps' relatively heavier lower limbs and lighter trunks (Zihlman 1984). The morphological differences in body proportions between the two species of chimps appear, therefore, to have very definite locomotor behavioural correlates; and they suggest a greater frequency and propensity for bipedal behaviour in pygmy than in common chimps.

The origin of hominid locomotion

The importance of bipedality as a defining hominid feature means that there is much interest in how the transition from a quadrupedal ape to a bipedal hominid might have taken place. The transformation has been assumed to have involved substantial morphological and behavioural change, and to have occurred when the apes came to the ground. A number of clues suggest that the origin of hominid bipedality involved more than simply coming to the ground. Rather, a two-step transition may have been involved—from the trees to the ground, and from ground-dwelling in forest or woodlands to ground-dwelling on the savannah—and this need not have led to a great deal of morphological change in its initial stages.

When molecular findings first reported that chimpanzees, gorillas, and humans had a common ancestor, Washburn (1968) concluded that this common ancestor was probably a knuckle-walking ape. This locomotor adaptation found in all African apes, he argued, would have provided a behavioural transition from the arboreal life of the ape ancestors, where climbing and hanging were important, to ground-dwelling on the savannah, which is characteristic of early hominids. This method of locomotion would have opened up new areas of feeding, by allowing animals to move between isolated trees and so live in and exploit areas other than a dense forest habitat. Thus, the first step towards bipedality was probably moving on the ground between groups of trees in an environment of fragmented, rather than dense tropical, forest. This idea fits very well with what is known about environmental change during the middle to late Miocene—a time between 5 and 10 Ma ago, when the dense tropical forests in East Africa were breaking up, resulting in a mosaic habitat with open woodlands and grasslands (Laporte and Zihlman 1983).

The second step in the origin of hominid bipedality was for these knuckle-walking apes to become mobile in an environment like the savannah mosaic, where trees are in discontinuous stands or clumps. I maintain that ground-dwelling in the forest is not the same as terrestrial locomotion in the savannah; rather these terrains and vegetation require different locomotor solutions to those in the forest.

Perhaps the answer to Susman's (1984, p. 390) key question—Why did early hominids elect a *bipedal* rather than a knuckle-walking solution to the problem of terrestriality?—involves several factors: the propensity for bipedality in the African apes, and especially the pygmy chimpanzees; an upper limb not well adapted for weight-bearing (Reynolds 1985a; 1985b); an omnivorous and opportunist diet (Bourlière 1985); and the necessity for mobility and long-distance travel to obtain food. If the combination of knuckle-walking and bipedal frequency possessed by pygmy chimpanzees was present in the common ancestor, then it is not difficult to imagine a transition to hominid bipedalism that initially involved minimal morphological change.

The hominid fossil record

What clues about the transition to hominid locomotion are found in the fossil record? From the South African and East African fossil sites have come all parts of the locomotor skeleton. In addition, two important clues to bipedality have emerged in the past decade: footprints and 'Lucy'. Footprints dated at about 3.5 Ma old are the oldest evidence of hominid bipedality. The individuals who made them had short, broad feet; the great toe might have been somewhat adducted. The prints are not identical to those of modern humans, but they are surprisingly similar, considering their great age.

The discovery of almost half a skeleton from Hadar, Ethiopia, added a new dimension to understanding the body build and proportions of 3 Ma-old ancestors—a *Gestalt* not possible to reconstruct from isolated and fragmentary limb bones. This skeleton demonstrates the uniqueness of the australopithecine body proportions. The nearly complete humerus and femur allow estimates of the ratio of humerus to femur length—84 in Lucy (A.L. 288), compared with 74 in modern humans, 98 in pygmy chimpanzees, and 101 in common chimpanzees (Johanson and Taieb 1976; Zihlman and Cramer 1978). This ratio, together with other measurements, indicate that

Lucy had a lower limb similar in length to chimps, but a shorter upper limb. The comparison suggests that if the ancestral form were similar to pygmy chimps in body build, then, during the shift from quadrupedal to bipedal locomotion, one of the earliest changes was reduction in length of the upper limbs and probably a reduction in their mass. This change would serve to lower the centre of gravity and make upright posture more stable (Zihlman and Lowenstein 1983).

In addition to the intermediate nature of limb-bone proportions, the morphology of several parts of the skeleton also appears 'intermediate' between chimpanzees and modern humans. For example, the ankle joint, and especially the talus, suggests greater mobility in fossil hominids than in modern humans; the toe bones are relatively longer and more curved; the thorax resembles that of the chimpanzees, and the ilium is less curved, like that of the chimps (Le Gros Clark 1947; Stern and Susman 1982; Schmid 1983; Susman *et al.* 1984). However, when the locomotor behaviour is reconstructed, the morphology demonstrates a fossil group of hominids in transition from a chimp-like ancestor towards the pattern found in modern humans. Given the age of early hominids compared with molecular estimates of divergence and the anatomical features of the locomotor system, pygmy chimps seem to be an excellent model for a bipedal precursor.

Testing the model

Studies on proteins and DNA of humans and African apes demonstrated their close genetic affinity and suggested a recent, three-way divergence about 5 Ma ago. These findings emphasized that the origin of hominids was linked both to chimpanzee and to gorilla origins. Therefore, a morphological model for the proposed common ancestor had to be suitable for all three species. Since the pygmy chimpanzee prototype for this common ancestor was proposed in 1978, new data and reinterpretations of fossil evidence, and new data on molecular relationships and on pygmy chimpanzee behaviour, have all contributed to modifying this original proposal. In this period, pygmy chimpanzees have become even more useful in formulating and testing hypotheses about human origins.

Firstly, new data and interpretations of the Miocene fossil record now suggest that there are no contenders for the immediate ancestor to *Australopithecus*. *Ramapithecus–Sivapithecus* fossils, the Miocene hominoids with thickly enamelled molar teeth, are believed by some to be related to the orang-utan (Andrews and Cronin 1982; Pilbeam 1982). A recent study on enamel microstructure demonstrates that enamel thickness of molar teeth is not an identifying hominid feature (Martin 1985; cf. Kay 1981).

Perhaps the most important new clues to the common ape–human ancestor are recent molecular data from DNA hybridization (Sibley and Ahlquist 1984) and mitochondrial DNA (Hasegawa *et al.* 1984), which discriminate the branching orders among closely related species. These two lines of evidence, as well as radio-immunoassay (Lowenstein 1984), suggest that chimpanzees are more closely related to humans than either group is to gorillas, a finding that strengthens the chimpanzee model. (See Fig. 6.8.)

In the light of this information, chimpanzee behaviour in general becomes more significant for understanding the behaviour of the ape–human common ancestor and of early hominids. Field studies of common chimps have provided a wealth of information on tool-using, diet and predation, and food-sharing, and they continue to be of great interest. In particular, recent studies by Boesch and Boesch (1983, 1984) on common chimpanzees of the Ivory Coast, reveal that they use anvils and several kinds of hammers to open five species of hard-shelled nuts, behaviours which require a great deal of skill and many years to master. Further studies of Mahale Mountain chimpanzees have documented increasing evidence of predation by females (Takahata *et al.* 1984), a behaviour thought previously to be almost exclusively male.

The growing body of information on wild and captive pygmy chimpanzees expands our knowledge of chimpanzee behaviour, and provides an additional basis for conceptualizing the ape–human ancestor and early hominid behaviour. With regard to diet, for example, pygmy chimpanzees, like common chimps, rely largely on fruit, with some predation and meat-eating (Badrian and Malenky 1984; Kano and Muluvwa 1984). However, there are some interesting departures. For example, they forage for earthworms on the forest floor and may dig for them in shallow streams and mud beds.

Food and feeding are a focus for social interactions, especially food sharing and sexual behaviour (Savage-Rumbaugh and Wilkerson 1978; Kano 1980). Plant food is frequently shared among all age–sex classes. The pattern of food-sharing contrasts with that known for common chimpanzees. In particular, adult females are donors over twice as frequently as adult males; and they share food with other adult females and with individuals other than their own offspring (Kano 1980; Kuroda 1984). Adult males rarely share food among themselves, and sexual behaviour often occurs in connection with food-sharing, especially for females' obtaining food from a male.

Pygmy chimpanzee social groups manifest the flexibility of common chimpanzee groups, but differ in having at least one adult of each sex in each group (Kuroda 1979; Kano 1982; Badrian and Badrian 1984). The core of the society seems to be strongly bonded females and the males associating with them (Kuroda 1979, Thompson-Handler *et al.* 1984). In contrast to the common chimpanzee pattern, where adult males frequently groom and interact, pygmy chimp males avoid each other and groom infrequently.

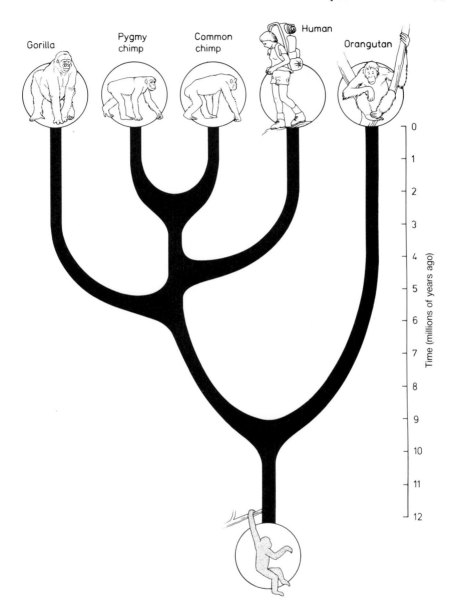

Fig. 6.8. Family tree of great apes and humans, based upon recent information from DNA.

Pygmy chimpanzee communication skills are of particular interest, in contrast to those of common chimps. Savage-Rumbaugh, who has worked extensively with both chimp species in the laboratory, first reported frequent food-sharing in association with sexual behaviour among pygmy chimps (Savage-Rumbaugh and Wilkerson 1978); and this has now been confirmed and elaborated among wild populations (Kano 1980; Kuroda 1984). Their sexual behaviour involves a greater number of possible postures, including front-to-front copulation, and the intended position is communicated between individuals through gestures and facial expressions (Savage-Rumbaugh *et al.* 1977).

In a study of spontaneous communication in a young pygmy chim, Kanzi, and his mother, Matata, at Yerkes Primate Center, Savage-Rumbaugh (1984) notes a number of contrasts with the common chimps, Sherman and Austin, with whom she has worked intensively for a number of years. In particular, she reports the development of non-verbal communication and documents the emergence of intentionality. Kanzi frequently combines gestures with vocalizations, which appear to be voluntary and used intentionally to draw attention to himself and his wants. Pointing at and touching objects, with visual checking and vocal signals, appeared spontaneously to express intentionality, behaviours not typical of common chimps. The mother Matata responds to Kanzi's communications as if they are intentional, something which common chimpanzee mothers do not do.

Conclusion

Hitherto, reconstructions of early hominids have tended to emphasize tools and predation, because of the preoccupation with stone tools and animal bones in the archaeological record. Less attention has been focused on social context and interaction. Pygmy chimps are important, not only for the anatomical and locomotor perspective they bring to the fossil record, but also because their social behaviour gives more clues about the social dimension in the origin of hominid behaviour. For example, discussions on the origin of bipedalism consistently emphasize carrying and using objects, displays, or moving around the environment. Yet the context of pygmy chimpanzee bipedalism is most frequently social, as reported by Mori (1984). Young pygmy chimpanzees are frequently bipedal in order to look into their mothers' faces (Kuroda, pers. comm.).

Thus, pygmy chimpanzees offer many clues to the nature of the 'missing link' between apes and humans. Not only do they add to our knowledge of chimpanzee behaviour, but also they broaden our understanding and underscore the importance of the social dimensions of behaviour. Pygmy chimps help envision how new patterns of foraging, food-sharing, social relationships, and communication might have emerged among early hominids.

Acknowledgements

I thank Catherine Borchert and Jerold Lowenstein for discussion and comments, Sue Savage-Rumbaugh for providing Figs 6.1 and 6.2, Carla Simmons for the illustrations, and the Faculty Research Committee and Division of Social Sciences, University of California, Santa Cruz, for financial assistance.

References

Andrews, P. (1981). Species diversity and diet in monkeys and apes during the Miocene. In *Aspects of human evolution*, (ed. C. Stringer), pp. 25–61. Taylor & Francis, London.

Andrews, P. and Cronin, J.E. (1982). The relationships of *Sivapithecus* and *Ramapithecus* and the evolution of the orang-utan. *Nature*, **297**, 541–6.

Badrian, A. and Badrian, N. (1984). Social organization of *Pan paniscus* in the Lomako Forest, Zaïre. In *The pygmy chimpanzee*, (ed. R.L. Susman), pp. 325–46. Plenum Press, New York.

Badrian, N. and Malenky, R.K. (1984). Feeding ecology of *Pan paniscus* in the Lomako forest, Zaïre. In *The pygmy chimpanzee*, (ed. R.L. Susman), pp. 275–99. Plenum Press, New York.

Boesch, C. and Boesch, H. (1983). Optimisation of nut-cracking with natural hammers by wild chimpanzees. *Behaviour*, **3/4**, 265–86.

Boesch, C. and Boesch, H. (1984). Possible causes of sex differences in the use of natural hammers by wild chimpanzees. *J. Hum. Evol.*, **13**, 415–40.

Bourlière, F. (1985). Primate communities: their structure and role in tropical ecosystems. *Int. J. Primat.* **6**, 1–26.

Broom, R. Robinson, J.T., and Schepers G. (1950). *Sterkfontein ape-man*. Plesianthropus, Transvaal Museum Memoir, 4, Pretoria.

Broom, R. and Robinson, J.T. (1952) *The Swartkrans ape-man*, Paranthropus crassidens. Transvaal Museum Memoir, 6, Pretoria.

Brown, W.M., Prager, E.M., Wang, A., and Wilson, A.C. (1982). Mitochondrial DNA sequences of primates: tempo and mode of evolution. *J. Mol. Evol.*, **18**, 225–39.

Coolidge, H.J. (1933). *Pan paniscus*, pygmy chimpanzee from south of the Congo River. *Amer. J. Phys. Anthrop.*, **18**, 1–59.

Coolidge, H.J. and Shea, B.T. (1982). External body dimensions of *Pan paniscus* and *Pan troglodytes* chimpanzees. *Primates*, **23**, 245–51.

Coppens, Y., Howell, F.C., Isaac, G.L., and Leakey, R.E.F. (1976). *Earliest man and environment in the Lake Rudolf Basin*. University of Chicago Press, Chicago.

Cramer, D.L. (1977). Craniofacial morphology of *Pan paniscus*. A morphometric and evolutionary appraisal. *Contrib. Primat.*, **10**, 1–64.

Cramer, D.L. and Zihlman A.L. (1978). Sexual dimorphism in the pygmy chimpanzee, *Pan paniscus*. In *Recent advances in primatology*, (ed. D.J. Chivers and K.A. Joysey), Vol. 3, pp. 487–90. Academic Press, New York.

Curtis, G.H. (1981). Establishing a relevant time scale in anthropological and archaeological research. *Phil. Trans. R. Soc. Lond.*, **B292**, 7–20.

Dart, R.A. (1925). *Australopithecus africanus*: the man-ape of South Africa. *Nature*, **115**, 195–9.

Dart, R.A. (1948). The Makapansgat proto-human *Australopithecus prometheus*. *Amer. J. Phys. Anthrop.*, n.s. **6**, 259–84.

Dart, R.A. (1949). The first pelvic bones of *Australopithecus prometheus*. *Amer. J. Phys. Anthrop.*, n.s. **7**, 255–7.

Darwin, C. (1859). *On the origin of species*. John Murray, London.

Darwin, C. (1871). *Descent of man and selection in relation to sex*. Murray, London.

Doolittle, R.F. (1979). Protein evolution. In *The proteins*, Vol. 4, H. Neurath and R.L. Hill Eds., Academic Press, New York, pp. 2–118.

Eckhardt, R. (1972). Population genetics and human evolution. *Scientific American*, **226** (1), 94–103.

Glen, W. (1982). *The road to Jaramillo. Critical years of the revolution in earth science*. Stanford University Press, Stanford.

Goodall, J. van Lawick (1968). The behaviour of free-living chimpanzees in the Gombe Stream Reserve. *Anim. Beh. Monogr.*, **1**, 161–311.

Goodall, J. van Lawick and Hamburg, D.A. (1975). Chimpanzee behaviour as a model for the behaviour of early man. In *Am. Handbook Psychiatry*, pp. 000–00. Basic Books, New York.

Goodman, M. (1963). Man's place in the phylogeny of the primates as reflected in serum proteins. In *Classification and human evolution*, (ed. S.L. Washburn), pp. 204–34, Aldine, Chicago.

Grand, T.I. (1977). Body weight: its relation to tissue composition, segment distribution, and motor function. I. Interspecific comparisons. *Am. J. Phys. Anthrop.*, **47**, 211–39.

Hasegawa, M., Yano, T., and Kishino, H. (1984). A new molecular clock of mitochondrial DNA and the evolution of hominoids. *Proc. Japan. Acad.*, **60B**, 95–8.

Huxley, T.H. (1863). *Evidence as to man's place in nature*. Williams & Norgate, London.

Johanson, D.C. and Edey, M. (1981). *Lucy: the beginnings of humankind*. Simon & Schuster, New York.

Johanson, D.C. and Taieb, M. (1976). Plio-Pleistocene discoveries in Hadar, Ethiopia. *Nature*, **260**, 293–7.

Jukes, T.H. (1980). Silent nucleotide substitutions and the molecular clock. *Science*, **210**, 973–8.

Jungers, W. and Susman, R.L. (1984). Body size and skeletal allometry in African apes. In *The pygmy chimpanzee*, (ed. R.L. Susman), pp. 131–77. Plenum, New York.

Kano, T. (1980). Social behaviour of wild pygmy chimpanzees (*Pan paniscus*) of Wamba: a preliminary report. *J. Hum. Evol.*, **9**, 243–60.

Kano, T. (1982). The social group of pygmy chimpanzees (*Pan paniscus*) of Wamba. *Primates*, **23** (2), 171–88.

Kano, T. and Mulavwa, M. (1984). Feeding ecology of the pygmy chimpanzees (*Pan paniscus*) of Wamba. In *The pygmy chimpanzee*, (ed. R.L. Susman), pp. 233–74. Plenum Press, New York.

Kay, R.F. (1981). The nut-crackers—a new theory of the adaptations of the Rama-pithecinae. *Am. J. Phys. Anthrop.*, **55**, 141–51.

Kinzey, W.G. (1984). The dentition of the pygmy chimpanzee, *Pan paniscus*. In *The pygmy chimpanzee*, (ed. R.L. Susman), pp. 65–88. Plenum Press, New York.

Kuroda, S. (1979). Grouping of the pygmy chimpanzees. *Primates*, **20**, 161–80.

Kuroda, S. (1984). Interaction over food among pygmy chimpanzees. In *The pygmy chimpanzee*, (ed. R.L. Susman), pp. 301–24. Plenum, New York.

Laitman, J.T. and Heimbuch, R.C. (1984). A measure of basicranial flexion in *Pan paniscus*, the pygmy chimpanzee. IN *The pygmy chimpanzee*, (ed. R.L. Susman), pp. 49–63. Plenum, New York.

Laporte, L.F. and Zihlman, A.L. (1983). Plates, climates and hominoid evolution. *S. Afr. J. Sci.*, **79**, 96–110.

Le Gros Clark, W.E. (1947). Observations on the anatomy of the fossil Australopi-thecinae. *J. Anat.*, **81**, 300–34.

Lewis, G.E. (1937). Taxonomic syllabus of Siwalik fossil anthropoids. *Am. J. Sci.*, **34**, 139–47.

Lowenstein, J.M. (1984). The molecular evidence: timing and branching order of human ancestors. Presented at 10th Int. Cong. Primat., Nairobi.

Lowenstein, J.M. and Zihlman A.L. (1984). Human evolution and molecular biology. *Persp. Biol. Med.*, **27**, 611–22.

Martin, L. (1985). Significance of enamel thickness in hominoid evolution. *Nature*, **314**, 260–3.

Mori, A. (1984). An ethological study of pygmy chimpanzees in Wamba, Zaïre: a comparison with chimpanzees. *Primates*, **25**, 255–78.

Pilbeam, D.L. (1978). Rearranging our family tree. *Hum. Nature* 1, 38–45.

Pilbeam, D.L. (1982). New hominoid skull material from the museums of Pakistan. *Nature*, **295**, 232–4.

Reader, R. (1981). *Missing links*. Little Brown, Boston.

Reynolds, T.R. (1985*a*). Mechanics of increased support of weight by the hindlimbs in Primates. *Am. J. Phys. Anthrop.*, **67**, 335–49.

Reynolds, T.R. (1985*b*). Stresses on the limbs of quadrupedal primates. *Am. J. Phys. Anthrop.*, **67**, 351–62.

Sarich, V.M. (1967). Man's place in Nature. Presented at the American Anthro-pological Association Annual Meetings, Washington D.C.

Sarich, V.M. and Cronin, J.E. (1976). Molecular systematics of the primates. In *Molecular anthropology*, (ed. M. Goodman and R.E. Tashian), pp. 141–70. Plenum, New York.

Sarich, V.M. and Wilson, A.C. (1967). Immunological time scale for hominid evolu-tion. *Science*, **1588**, 1200–3.

Savage-Rumbaugh, E.S. (1984). *Pan paniscus* and *Pan troglodytes*: contrasts in preverbal communicative competence. In *The pygmy chimpanzee*, (ed. R.L. Susman), pp. 395–413. Plenum, New York.

Savage-Rumbaugh, E.S. and Wilkerson, B.J. (1978). Socio-sexual behaviour in *Pan paniscus* and *Pan troglodytes*: a comparative study. *J. Hum. Evol.*, 7, 327–44.

Savage-Rumbaugh, E.S., Wilkerson, B.J., and Bakeman, R. (1977). Spontaneous gestural communication among conspecifics in the pygmy chimpanzee (*Pan paniscus*). In *Progress in ape research*, (ed. G.H. Bourne), pp. 97–116. Academic Press, New York.

Schmidt, P. (1983). Ein Rekonstruktion des Skelettes von A.L. 288-1 (Hadar) und deren Konsequenzen. *Folia Primat.*, **40**, 283–306.

Schwartz, J.H. (1984). The evolutionary relationships of man and orangutans. *Nature*, **308**, 501–5.

Schwarz, E. (1929). Das Vorkommen des Schimpansen auf den linken Kongo-Ufer. *Rev. Zool. Bot. Afr.*, **XVI** (4), 425–6.

Shea, B.T. (1981). Relative growth of the limbs and trunk in the African apes. *Am. J. Phys. Anthrop.* **56**, 179–201.

Sibley, C.G. and Ahlquist, J.E. (1984). The phylogeny of the hominoid primates, as indicated by DNA–DNA hybridization. *J. Mol. Evol.*, **20**, 2–15.

Sigmon, B.A. and Cybulski, J. (1981). Homo erectus. *Papers in honor of Davidson Black*. University of Toronto Press, Toronto.

Simons, E.L. (1961). *The phyletic position of* Ramapithecus. Postilla, Peabody Mus., No. 57. Yale University, New Haven.

Simons, B.A. (1968). A source for dental comparison of *Ramapithecus* with *Australopithecus* and *Homo*. *S. Afr. J. Sci.* **64**, p. 92.

Simons, B.A. (1981). Man's immediate forerunners. *Phil. Trans. R. Soc. London*, **B292**, 21–41.

Simons, E.L. and Pilbeam, D.R. (1972). Hominoid paleoprimatology. In *The functional and evolutionary biology of primates*, (ed. R.H. Tuttle), pp. 36–62. Aldine-Atherton, Chicago.

Stern, J.T. and Susman, R.L. (1983). The locomotor anatomy of *Australopithecus afarensis*. *Am. J. Phys. Anthrop.*, **60**, 279–318.

Susman, R.L. (1984). The locomotor behavior of *Pan paniscus* in the Lomako Forest. In *The pygmy chimpanzee*, (ed. R.L. Susman), pp. 369–93. Plenum Press, New York.

Susman, R.L., Badrian, N.L., and Badrian, A.J. (1980). Locomotor behaviour of *Pan paniscus* in Zaïre. *Am. J. Phys. Anthrop.*, **53**, 69–80.

Susman, R.L., Stern, J.T., and Jungers, W.L. (1984). Arboreality and bipedality in the Hadar hominids. *Folia Primat.*, **43**, 113–56.

Takahata, Y., Hasegawa, T., and Nishida, T. (1984). Chimpanzee predation in the Mahale Mountains from August 1979 to May 1982. *Int. J. Primat.*, **5**, 213–33.

Thompson-Handler, N., Malenky, R. and Badrian, N. (1984). Sexual behavior of *Pan paniscus* under natural conditions in the Lomako Forest, Equateur, Zaïre. In *The pygmy chimpanzee*, (ed. R.L. Susman), pp. 347–68. Plenum Press, New York.

Tratz, E. and Heck, H. (1954). Der afrikanische anthropoide 'Bonobo,' eine neue Nemschenaffengattung. *Saugetierkd. Mitt.*, **2**, 97–101.

Washburn S.L. (1951). The analysis of primate evolution with particular reference to the origin of man. *Cold Spring Harbor Symp. Quant. Biol.*, **15**, 67–78.

Washburn, S.L. (1968). *The study of human evolution*. Condon Lectures, Oregon State System of Higher Education. Eugene, Oregon.

Weiner, J.S., Oakley, K.P., and Le Gros Clark, W.E. (1953). The solution of the Piltdown problem. *Bull. Br. Mus. Nat. Hist.*, **A2** (3), 141–6.

Wilson, A.C., Carlson, S.S., and White, T.J. (1977). Biochemical evolution. *Ann. Rev. Biochem.*, **46**, 573–639.

Yunis, J.J. and Prakash, O. (1982). The origin of man. *Science*, **215**, 1525–30.

Zihlman, A.L. (1976). Sexual dimorphism and its behavioural implications in early hominids. In *Les plus anciens hominides*, (ed. P.V. Tobias and Y. Coppens), pp. 268–93, Colloque VI, IX Union Internationale des Sciences Prehistoriques et Protohistoriques, Nice. CNRS, Paris.

Zihlman, A.L. (1980). Locomotor behaviour in pygmy and common chimpanzees. *Am. J. Phys. Anthrop.*, **52**, p. 295 (abstract).

Zihlman, A.L. (1983). A behavioral reconstruction of *Australopithecus*. In *Hominid origins. Inquiries past and present*, (ed. K.J. Reichs), pp. 207–38. University Press of the Americas, Washington DC.

Zihlman, A.L. (1984). Body build and tissue composition in *Pan paniscus* and *Pan troglodytes*, with comparisons to other hominoids. In *The pygmy chimpanzee*, (ed. R.L. Susman), pp. 179–200. Plenum Press, New York.

Zihlman, A.L. and Cramer, D.L. (1978). Skeletal differences between pygmy (*Pan paniscus*) and common chimpanzees (*Pan troglodytes*). *Folia Primatol.*, **29**, 86–94.

Zihlman, A.L., Cronin, J.E., Cramer, D.L., and Sarich, V.M. (1978). Pygmy chimpanzees as a possible prototype for the common ancestor of humans, chimpanzees and gorillas. *Nature*, **275**, 744–6.

Zihlman, A.L. and Lowenstein, J.M. (1979). False start of the human parade. *Nat. Hist.*, **88**, 86–91.

Zihlman, A.L. and Lowenstein, J.M. (1983). *Ramapithecus* and *Pan paniscus*: significance for human origins. In *New interpretations of ape and human ancestry*, (ed. R.L. Ciochon and R.S. Corruccini), pp. 677–94. Plenum, New York.

7

Cutting and carrying: archaeology and the emergence of the genus Homo

Glynn Isaac

Introduction

It was a great pleasure to come to Oxford to participate in the lecture series on 'Human Origins', and to represent the contribution of archaeology to the study of human evolution. The preceding chapters are principally by physical anthropologists and human anatomists. They have shown you something of the physical appearance of the succession of human ancestors, if not in the field then at least in the bone. My concern is with ascertaining how some of these creatures conducted aspects of their lives. I will start by recapitulating the fossil evidence. This will raise some general issues that I will address later. After this recapitulation I will attempt to orient the discussion by comparing humans with their closest living relatives, the chimpanzees, thus establishing some crucial differences. Next I will consider what use we can make of modern ecological studies, as these may provide information for our interpretation of the past. Then I will look at the actual stratified record, and more specifically at the archaeological record. Finally, I will consider the implications of all this evidence for our understanding of human evolution.

For the last 10 or 12 years I have been involved, together with a large team of colleagues, in an investigation of a whole series of novelties which appeared in the stratigraphic record about two million years ago. These novelties are associated with, or seen in, the first fossils which my taxonomic colleagues, in their wisdom, put into the genus *Homo*. In general terms, these are the first fossils that show enlarged brains. How these creatures were actually using their increased brain, the fossils themselves do not tell us, but I am going to argue that archaeology can help to provide some insight. In addition, I shall stress that in order to understand the record of the past, people who are interested in human evolution will have to know a lot more about the way in which the African savannah is structured. This information is essential if we are to know what problems and opportunities our ancestors faced. The questions that need to be asked cannot be answered in a library; they have to be taken out into the savannah, albeit with some advice from ecological colleagues, and then, like the elephant's child, the researcher finds out for himself. Over the next ten to twenty years, this kind of study is going to be a burgeoning field of inquiry. Moreover, it is going to be an entirely open-ended field. There are only a limited number of Olduvais, and Koobi Foras, and Hadars, and not everyone who is interested in human evolution can get the chance to dig in one of these places; but there really is a virtually unlimited opportunity for applied ecological studies. So if there are bright young people who are looking for opportunities to make contributions to science and become famous, this is a golden opportunity for them.

There is a final point to be made in this introduction. In our understanding of human evolution, there has been increasing concern in recent years, not only to know the sequence of stages by which modern humans came into existence, but also to understand the processes which initiated change; that is, we wish to understand evolutionary dynamics. The ecological approach that I am advocating is an essential part of this dynamical approach to the question of human origins.

General issues arising out of a recapitulation of the fossil evidence

In strata that are older than eight million years, dating to the late Miocene, there is a lot of fragmentary material which comes from comparatively large hominoids; we know that there were many different species, indeed many different genera of hominoids. It used to be believed that you could pick from this variety one particular genus which was the ancestor of later hominids; but most wise scholars now recognize that there is an interesting diversity and that we really cannot choose which ones are ancestral. Indeed, it is almost certain that we have not yet found the actual ancestors of later hominids. Between eight million and four million years ago, we have very little evidence indeed, just a few tantalizing fragments, mostly from the East African Rift. There is enough to suggest that Elaine Morgan is probably incorrect, and that our ancestors probably were not living on the edge of the sea at that time. Almost certainly, they were living in the East African savannah environment. However, virtually nothing is known about their anatomical characteristics, or about their ways of life during those four million years.

Yet by four million years ago, things had happened! Around the three and three-quarter to four million year mark, there is a fairly abundant fossil record that makes it absolutely clear that at least one group of hominids had made a key transition: they had become upright bipedal creatures. This means that they had modified their posture and locomotion, and were wandering around, perhaps between groves of trees, in comparatively open country. This uprightness challenges our understanding of the term 'human', because if we saw these creatures at a distance of one hundred yards we would be puzzled; we would say, 'We know what those are; those are humans.' This is because there is nothing else that moves like us on the face of the Earth. However, at closer quarters we would see an ape's head on top of a distinctively human-like body. Not only is the brain ape-size but, if the creature could be tempted to open its mouth, to our surprise we would see extraordinarily large teeth. No modern humans or other primates have brains or teeth like these *Australopithecines*. Clearly, by four million years ago something quite extraordinary had begun to happen.

By two million years ago, more novelties appear, including the first fossils called by us *Homo habilis*. These show brains significantly larger than apes, but within essentially ape-size bodies. Now we find the first stones that have been deliberately broken to create sharp-edged implements. Also for the first time, we find places where there are concentrations of stone tools and broken-up animal bones; and among the bones we find some with cut-marks on them. The other interesting and distinctive feature of this two million year time-band is that this is the only period where, within the same sedimentary basin, we find more than one species of upright bipedal creature. There are multiple species of hominids: scientists argue whether there are two, three, or four species; but there are certainly at least two. This is the only time in the geological past when, if you were one kind of hominid wandering around the landscape, from time to time you would observe another upright bipedal creature who belonged to a different species. This situation prevailed from just before two million years ago until around one million years ago, and then the pattern shifted to the situation where, as far as we know, only one hominid existed at once, and certainly only ever one in any given region.

After two million years, we find fossils which have a very characteristic appearance: the brain volume is not much changed from those first enlarged brains of *Homo habilis*; but the format of the skull has changed. As previous chapters in this book have illustrated, hominids younger than two million years have very distinctive skulls, with massive brow ridges and elongate low brain vaults. This format is characteristic of *Homo erectus*, and lasts, albeit with variations on the theme, from one-and-a-half million years ago essentially until the last major shift in the fossil record, which occurs at a mere 40 000 years ago. Then, what I like to call 'the loss of robusticity transition' took place. Up until that transition, all hominids were, by our standards, immensely muscle-bound, strong, and burly creatures. About 40 000 years ago, however, modern types of physique became predominant, together, of course, with a tremendous burgeoning of cultural elaboration.

This rather lengthy preamble is intended to put in context the piece of the stratigraphic record that I have been dealing with in my archaeological research over the past few years. Now, having reached the present, I want to identify some of the distinctively human traits that were acquired on our journey, by comparing us with other modern primates.

Comparisons between great apes and humans

Table 7.1 sets out some of the distinctions between humans and their closest living relatives, the chimpanzees. The anatomical distinctions include the fact that humans are upright bipeds, whereas chimpanzees and gorillas are quadrupedal knuckle-walkers. By mammalian standards (indeed by the standards of the whole animal kingdom), all of the large hominids have large brains; but humans have particularly large brains. This, of course, is one of the things of which we are especially proud. In terms of physiology, the chimpanzees have a conspicuous oestrus cycle, (i.e. females come on heat), whereas humans have concealed ovulation: (i.e. there is no conspicuous coming on heat). Humans have reduced canines, and chimpanzees have extraordinary thick grinding molars, though they are less extreme than those of our australopithecine ancestors.

Table 7.1. Distinctions between humans and chimpanzees

CLR (Chimpanzee)	Modern humans
Quadrupedal (knuckle-walkers)	Bipeds
Large-brained primates	Very large brains
Conspicuous oestrus	Concealed ovulation
Large Canines	Reduced canines
	Thick-enamel, grinding molars
	Carrying
Tool use	Tool-dependent
Some meat eaten	Meat-eating maximized
Feed-as-you-go	CPF—radial movements
	—division of labour
	—'home base'
	—provisioning/food-sharing
	Marriage
	Reciprocal Obligations
	Language

These anatomical and physiological differences are interesting, but the list of behavioural distinctions is much longer and, I would argue, in a certain sense much more important. Humans, for example, are utterly dependent on the use of tools and equipment; and in many cultures they appear to maximize their consumption of meat and other flesh. We know now that chimpanzees use tools, but their way of life does not depend on tool-use; and we know now that chimpanzees hunt and eat meat, but by comparison with humans this is a much more minor behaviour.

If we were interviewing a chimpanzee about what he thought was distinctive in humans, I am sure he would not start with the big brain, or with the use of tools. He would start with the fact that very often when humans get food, instead of eating it on the spot and then going to the next place, they pop the food into a bag and carry it somewhere else, often to share it with others. At that amazing occurrence, our chimpanzee would say, 'Would you believe it, they actually hand it over to another individual!' Food collection and sharing are the characteristic behaviours of what zoologists know as central-place foragers, and there are a whole set of crucial differences between humans and other great apes, that turn on the fact that, alone amongst primates, humans are central-place foragers. Typically, they undertake radial movement from some kind of base of operation, with members of the same social group going out in different directions for a portion of a day, or a couple of days. They then return and pool at least part of the food. Humans characteristically have a division of labour that is associated with this pattern. Not all adult members of society perform exactly the same food acquisition functions and other tasks. They have an agreed meeting-place that may move every couple of days, every couple of weeks, or every couple of years; but they have a place to which they can return, a place which we can call a home-base, a camp-site, a settlement, or whatever. This home-base is the place to which food is brought and given to young, to mates, and to other members of society, often (though not always) kin.

Having emphasized one particularly crucial difference between humans and other great apes, we may briefly consider two more. Humans have a very distinctive behaviour pattern which is universal in all human societies that we know about, for which the good old word 'marriage' is best. Males and females are linked by bonds that involve more than access to reproductive opportunity; there are reciprocal obligations and expectations in terms of supply of food and care. Further, human societies involve complex extended networks of reciprocal obligation amongst their members, that are calculated far off into the future. In a sense, humans play chess with their obligations.

Finally, we come to language. Language is the difference that our species is most proud of, and indeed it pervades the whole of human life. Whatever their anatomy, we would probably not agree to recognize other organisms as human if they did not use language and the whole system of thinking and symbolizing that goes with it.

These are some of the major differences that have arisen over the past five or ten million years of human evolution. My concern is to try to discover by what stages, under what ecological circumstances, and by what evolutionary mechanisms, this differentiation has taken place. Long ago, Charles Darwin suggested that the first event in human evolution was leaving the trees; but without a fossil record, he could only suggest a configuration of elements that might account for the development of humans' extraordinary abilities. He suggested that the use of tools and weapons had been important, and that various kinds of social interaction (and especially co-operation) had been important in creating linguistic skills and what he termed the moral sense. The really major advance since Darwin has been the discovery of a fossil record and an archaeological record. With the help of these records, we begin to perceive the processes that differentiated us from the apes. One of the great challenges facing palaeoanthropology, in my view, is figuring out how the australopithecines made their living: I am convinced that they had an adaptive mode that we do not yet understand. We may come nearer to understanding that vanished mode, by studying the ecology of modern savannah communities.

Ecological considerations

Darwin's crucial first event of leaving the trees involves a move from forest to savannah. The term 'savannah' is a conveniently loose one; I use it to mean those areas of Africa which have vegetation patterns that are neither dense tropical rain forest, on the one hand, nor desert, on the other. Savannahs involve comparatively open terrain with a reasonable extent of grass, and variable but incomplete tree cover. I argue that in a certain sense, humans, but probably not australopithecines, have adopted a bird-like solution as to how to live in the savannah. Let me explain.

Most biologists trying to think about evolutionary shifts would consider that one of the first places to start is with the nature of the food consumed and its distribution in the environment. These basic constraints dictate the options for organisms in solving the problem of obtaining food. Knowing what the options are is not going to explain the whole of an organism, but it is a good place to start. Let us look at some of these options in relation to the problem of human evolution.

Human evolution involved a transition from ancestors who were arboreal, forest- and woodland-living creatures, into descendants who were ground-dwelling, savannah-living creatures. It is clear from the fossil record that this was a transition that our ancestors had made by around four million years ago. In a forest there is a tremendously large mass of vegetation, which includes fruiting and tender foliage. Within a comparatively small space, there is a good deal of food suitable for primates, or at least for primates small enough not to fall off the ends of the branches where much of the food is located. This explains why primates are characteristically smallish mammals which eat fruit and tender leaves. There are lots of monkeys that answer to this description. The only two forest primates that do not are: first, the gorilla, which is enormous by primate standards, and which lives essentially on the ground in peculiar patches of very dense undergrowth amounting to huge salad bowls; and secondly, the orang-utan, which is both big and arboreal in ways that I, for one, do not fully understand. Chimpanzees are interesting: they are medium-sized by hominoid standards, and they are primarily frugivores, though they also eat leaves and other things; they tend to live in woodland, moving within the trees and on the ground between the trees; and their feeding is mostly done in trees.

The only two major primate adaptations to the savannah proper are found in the baboon and the patas monkey. The baboon is a small- to medium-sized, highly omnivorous monkey that eats fruit, leaves, grass stems, insects, and (when it can get them) live birds and mammals. It has been argued that, given this kind of diet, the baboon could not really be any bigger than it is, without coming into head on competition with the creatures who have really made the grassland savannahs their own, namely the ruminant ungulants. The baboon is believed to be at the limit of size for a non-ruminating creature that is not really enormous, like the rhinoceros and the elephant, at which size, other factors come into play. The other savannah form is the patas monkey, which is a highly selective feeder upon insects, fruits, seeds, and, to a lesser degree, leaves and little oozes of gum. The patas monkey is comparatively small and very mobile.

In thinking about human evolution, we have to confront the problem of the viability of a medium-sized, savannah-adapted animal. The early hominids appear to have weighed forty to sixty kilograms; that is, significantly more than baboons and patas monkeys. At this sort of size, there are real issues about what foods can sustain life and what kinds of ranging patterns will suffice to obtain them. If you live in a forest, the fruit and foliage is comparatively closely packed and you do not have to move large distances between feeding bouts. This is still true for animals like chimpanzees: a community of chimpanzees lives and dies within an area that would be an order of magnitude smaller than for most humans. This is because they do not need to travel so far to obtain the food that they require. But of course, by moving out of the forest, the early hominids were leaving behind a fruit- and foliage-dominated diet.

If the hominids did not eat fruit or foliage, what else was there? Seeds are characteristically quite small, though highly nutrient concentrated; nuts are a little larger and highly concentrated in nutrients; insects, again, are nutrient concentrated, but often small. These are different classes of food, all in small packets, which are typically utilized by primates; but in the savannah there are other options as well. First of all, there are underground plant storage options: tubers and bulbs. These tend to occur in quite large concentrations (that is, they are locally abundant) and they are nutrient rich. Secondly, there is meat; the savannah sustains a particularly large mass of moderate-to-big animals, and of course these also combine the qualities of local abundance and high nutrient value. I suggest that a major feature of the critical two-million-year-old shift in human evolution was a move by the hominids from an ape-type feeding regime of foliage and fruit, into a human-type feeding regime which involved increasing dependence on tubers and meat. This shift implies the introduction of new kinds of apparatus and new kinds of activities suited to the new pattern of food consumption.

At this point I want to introduce a newly fashionable approach to the study of food acquisition, which is called optimal foraging theory. This may sound rather grand, but in essence it is quite simple. Optimal foraging theory analyses the processes of life as a budget, in which the benefits on one side are weighed against the costs incurred in getting access to them on the other. The benefits are nutrients and energy gained; and the costs are the energy spent in searching for, or chasing, suitable food, eating, digestion, and perhaps detoxification. Today, ecologists are trying to understand the feeding strategies of extinct species in these terms. They focus on questions such as how animals may have evolved better ways of cutting search costs, locomotor costs, and so on. Can this approach throw any light on human origins?

An animal with almost no memory, that lives in a world where food is scattered about, has to wander around until it locates a food item; wander on until it locates another one; and so on. This is a very simple and primitive foraging strategy, and in fact many higher mammals do much better. In a variety of ways (through personal experience, learning from others within their social group, and so on), they have access to information about where food is likely to be. In this way, they are able to move smoothly and efficiently from one food source to another. I am going to argue that an extension of this behaviour was involved in human evolution.

Many monkeys forage in groups, which move purposefully from one food patch to another in ways that reveal some knowledge of where the patches are located. Two of the great apes, however, have quite different foraging patterns. In the case of the orang-utan, the females simply range in a small area of dense patches which is sufficient to feed their young and themselves, while the males try to patrol a larger area which includes several females, thus maintaining exclusive breeding access. The chimpanzee has essentially the same system. Females have their own individual feeding areas, but unlike orangs they socialize at times; and males do not go around singly as in the orangs, but rather in mafia-like gangs which seek to control the area and patrol the terrain in which the females live. In the chimpanzee there are strong continuing social relations, not only amongst the males, but also between them and the females of their area.

The human solution has been quite different. If you live in the savannah, where nutrient-rich food is generally widely dispersed, then you are faced with potentially large locomotor costs. There are several possible solutions to this problem. One, which has worked extremely well for the birds, is flying; but this demands a relatively small body size coupled with highly selective feeding. A second solution is to become so effective as a predator that nutrient benefits exceed locomotive costs; and a third is to become so effective at scanning the environment that scattered food sources can be effectively located. Vultures, for example, can spot carrion from ten or fifteen miles away, and then their energy-saving flight enables them to get to it with the minimum of locomotor costs.

None of these solutions were really open to the early hominids colonizing the savannah. Instead, they adopted a strategy which is far from being unique to humans: they exchanged information; and they shared food. By sharing the labour of scouting out a wide area, a co-operative social system may enable each of its members to do better than individuals who are not members of such an information-sharing club. Similarly, by sharing the surplus of their takings with others in return for reciprocal favours in the future, the members of a co-operative social system may each benefit in the long run. In each case, being in the sharing club is better than being out of it.

This, of course, is the kind of solution to the problem of food gathering which has been adopted by the social insects; and it is certainly how modern humans characteristically conduct their lives. I believe that there is a strong possibility that by about two million years ago, early hominids had shifted over to a foraging pattern adapted to widely dispersed, high-quality food, which involved a combination of information-exchange and sharing of surplus food taken in their ranging trajectory. Whether for hunter-gatherers, farmers, or modern city-dwellers, there is a central place, or home base, from which members of the same social group radiate into the surrounding area. Characteristically, members of the group may feed as they go; but equally characteristically, they may also bring back their surplus takings, pool them, and consume them collectively and socially in the central place. This is an extremely distinctive pattern within the primate order. Social insects do it; many birds do it; and some social carnivores do it. But among the primates, humans alone do it, whether out on the savannah or in the high-rise city apartment.

On the savannah, one of the major food sources that offers the opportunity to engage in food-sharing is the bodies of substantial dead animals. We are now in a phase of research where it is necessary for investigators to go out and actually get quantitative information on the scale and characteristics of these opportunities. Fortunately, this is beginning to happen. One of our students at Berkeley, Rob Blumenschine, has spent a year in the Serengeti, studying the frequency and spacing in the landscape of scavenging opportunities. Only when we know what kind of food would be available to hominids seeking to exploit these opportunities, will we be able to make realistic models. Another class of food which is distinctive to the savannah is plants which tuck away substantial stores of nutrients below the ground, out of reach of most animals. Here, even quite simple tools would enable hominids to exploit a major new food source. One of our students from

Australia, Anne Vincent, has been working in the African savannah, collecting quantitative information about the characteristics of this feeding opportunity.

Stratified evidence

I turn now to my own special interest, which is the stratified evidence. It was a very simple discovery that put archaeologists in business by allowing them to investigate aspects of human behaviour in the past. This discovery, made somewhere around two million years ago, was that by banging two stones together you can simply and effectively create a large supply of useful cutting implements. Two kinds of objects are made when stones are banged together: sharp slivers, which are known as flakes (these have knife-like qualities); and sharp-edged blocks from which flakes have been removed, which are known as cores. Archaeologists have given most of their attention to the rather fancier looking cores. These they call tools, and they lovingly name them choppers, discoids, and so on. But some of us are now beginning to think that it is probably the sharp-edged, knife-like flakes that are really important in terms of their adaptive significance for early hominids.

It has been shown that you can teach an ape to bang stones together to create sharp-edged fragments. However, ordinarily, apes do not make stone tools. Before the process of making flakes could become a habit, there had to be some function which was facilitated by having sharp edges available. Clearly, around two million years ago there was something in the lives of our ancestors that was made possible, or at least easier, by being able to generate sharp edges. For cores and flakes appear quite suddenly in the stratified sediments, and very rapidly they become exceedingly common objects. Presumably, the discovery of tool-making occurred by accident and then caught on because of its very great usefulness. Very soon, it seems that the hominids were flaking stones all over the landscape.

This, of course, puts archaeologists in business. In our research, we search the bad, eroding landscapes where the stratified evidence is exposed, looking for sharp-edged flakes and pieces of broken bone dribbling down the side of a hill. It is possible to follow a trail upwards to the point from which the artefacts and bones are originating. Then, once a site is found, we dig in squares until we reveal what would have been the surface of the ground one-and-a-half million years ago. What we have are grubby, dirty-brown, dusty holes in the ground. Their appearance is nothing like that when they formed; nonetheless, they are little windows on to a landscape which would have looked very much like Fig. 7.1. Now the hard work really starts. The position of each sharp stone flake, or core, or broken bone, is marked by a little white flag. The sort of material that is uncovered is very unlovely stuff; it is not going to

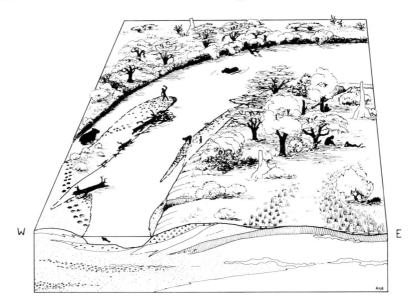

Fig. 7.1. Sketch by A.K. Behrensmeyer indicating the palaeotopography of a site (FxJj 50) at Koobi Fora, Kenya. The stratification provides the evidence for the reconstruction. Examples of some tree genera represented in the pollen are shown and marked: C = *Commiphora*, F = *Ficus* and S = *Salvadora*. Other trees are three species of *Acacia*.

win any prizes in an art show, and it makes very poor competition with the Tutankhamen exhibit. But it excites the Palaeolithic archaeologist nonetheless. For the patches of sharp flakes and broken bones, literally thousands of them within an area smaller than a living-room, provide us with one of the main documents that testifies to the way of life of our ancestors on the African savannah, between one and two million years ago.

In 1979, the BBC persuaded us to put back on to the floor of an excavation the results of nine months' digging, so that a film could be made of all the debris. I was very nervous, but we did learn something from the exercise. The ground surface had been littered with broken stones and bones, and there was no question that the stones were imported and broken by hominids. Fig. 7.2 shows a density plot of bone and a density plot of artefacts. With the help of the Malawi geologist, Zefe Kaufulu, we have been able to make a very precise reconstruction of the situation. The patch of bone and stones that we see in Fig. 7.3 is about 15 m in diameter, and it occurs right in the bend of a little river with vegetation along its banks, a stream channel with stones available near at hand. We found the casts of termites' nests in these same layers.

There is a very vigorous argument going on amongst archaeologists today

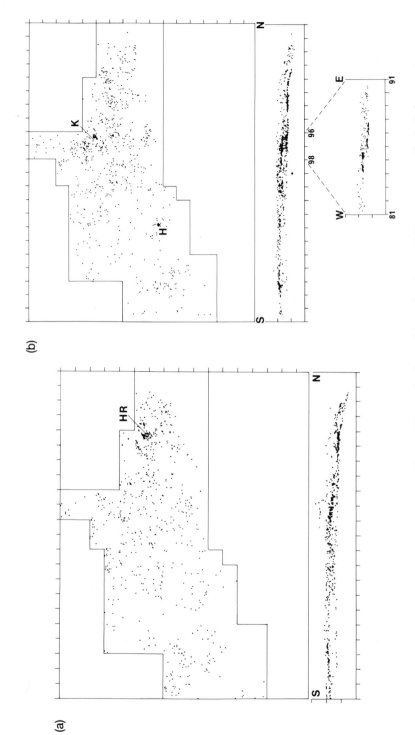

Fig. 7.2. a. The positions of plotted fragments of bone. HR marks the position of a cluster of hippopotamus rib shaft fragments. (Site FxJj 50) b. The positions of plotted stone artefacts. (Site FxJj 50)

Fig. 7.3.   Glynn Isaac at Koobi Fora in 1979. He is standing within the site of FxJj 50. The artefacts and broken bones have been replaced according to the horizontal co-ordinates taken during excavating.

about how such patches of stones, artefacts, and bones actually formed. We need to test alternative hypotheses against one another in an attempt to falsify them. For instance, one hypothesis has it that the artefacts and bones were washed together by streams; another has it that they were formed by the independent action of carnivores, with the hominids having nothing to do with the bones; another has it that the hominids took advantage of bones that carnivores had accumulated; and yet another that animals repeatedly came and died conveniently in the same place, thus providing an opportunity for hominids to scavenge. Finally, there is my favourite hypothesis, namely that these sites represent some kind of fossil central-place or home-base, to which hominids repeatedly carried food for consumption and stones for various tasks. Doubtless, the argument between these hypotheses will go on for some time to come; but it is hard now to escape the conclusion that the hominids were repeatedly carrying stones to these places in some quantity, and it seems overwhelmingly probable that they carried a good many of the bones as well.

Trying to understand the tools is the first priority. One of my colleagues, Nick Toth, who is an avid stone knapper, set out to replicate all of the kinds of tools which we had dug up, in order both to understand their form and to discover experimentally what kinds of uses they are good for. It takes a little bit of patience, but a branch usable as a spear or digging stick can be cut off a tree with simple flakes of the kind we find in the early hominid sites. Nick Toth has also demonstrated that you can use a simple lava flake to cut up a goat. Sometimes these experiments get out of hand. One year, just as I was preparing to go to East Africa, the telephone rang and someone said, 'I'm phoning from Colorado, and we have got a dead elephant here'. I said, 'Oh yes . . .'. He said, 'You have been saying that these early stone tools are for cutting up animals, and we think you should come and try to see if they really do.' I was unable to go, but Nick went and demonstrated that these tools will indeed cut through the hide of the biggest pachyderm. Once through the hide, of course, a really substantial quantity of meat becomes accessible. This is important, because surprising as it may seem, many large carnivores and scavengers of Africa are unable to break through the hide of the big pachyderms when they die. In other words, access to this kind of meat really may have been a vacant niche for tool-wielding early hominids.

The experiments which I have just mentioned show us some of the things that these simple early stone tools *can* do; but obviously, what really interests us is their actual use. For this, a new technique of analysis has emerged which, though not applicable to the lava from which most of the tools are made, can be used on the chert and flint-like rocks of which a minority of artefacts are composed. It turns out that a polish develops on these rocks in use, and that the kind of polish is distinctive of the kind of material being cut: meat, hide, soft plant-tissue, wood, and so on. We have used polish analysis on a sample of stone tools from an early site at Koobi Fora. Our results indicate that four specimens were being used for cutting meat, two for whittling wood, and two for cutting some kind of plant tissue. The first two uses were more or less what we expected, though the supporting evidence was of course welcome; but the last use is the one that puzzles us, and we are as yet uncertain as to what it may mean.

The bones at these early archaeological sites are found in very large quantities, and we have played a kind of jigsaw puzzle with some of them. Fig. 7.4 shows a bone reassembled from pieces that had been smashed apart with a hammerstone from site FxJj 50. Another of my colleagues, Henry Bunn, did an experiment for the BBC which involved breaking up a cow humerus using a stone as a hammer. The cow humerus broke in very much the same way as had our fossil example. In other words, the fragments illustrated in Fig. 7.4 are highly credible as hammer-fractured bone. When we looked carefully at the articular end from the same bone our hearts beat a little faster; for there were parallel lines on the lateral surface of the bone which looked exactly like

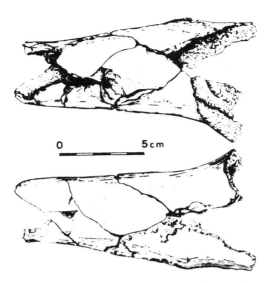

Fig. 7.4. Seven pieces of bone which fit back together to form the shaft of the humerus of a large bovid. The shaft seems to have been shattered by hammer blows.

score-marks made by a knife-like stone tool, cutting through tendons and separating the joint at the lower end of the humerus. This is clear evidence that the hominids were involved in cutting carcasses.

Finally, let me mention briefly one more class of evidence which has come to the fore recently. For some years we have known of single specimens from Olduvai and from Sterkfontein which consist of bones with sharpened ends and a peculiar polish. These specimens were classified as bone tools, although nobody knew what to make of them. In the last few years, several dozen more of these 'bone tools' have been found by the anthropologist Bob Brain in excavations at Swartkrans aged about 1.5 to 1.75 million years. Bob sent his young children out on to the hillside with comparable, but as yet unpolished bones, and said, 'Dig up bulbs like the baboons do!' When his children came back, lo and behold, the bones had polish on them that was indistinguishable from the archaeological specimens. I am quite confident that we have specific archaeological evidence of digging tubers and bulbs at 1.6 million years.

Conclusion

Returning to our list of contrasts between modern humans and their close living relatives, we can see that some of the behaviours that distinguish humans from chimpanzees began to make their presence felt around two million years ago. Certainly, at about that time hominids were carrying things about on a scale that no other living non-human primate does; certainly, also, they were involved in tool-use on a scale unmatched by any other living primate; and certainly too, they were eating meat. We do not know how often these hominids ate meat—whether it was once a lifetime, once a year, or once a week; but they were eating meat from very large animals on a scale that no other non-human primate does. It is not proven, but I would urge that we have reasonable evidence that the hominids had begun behaviours that either were central-place foraging, or at least were beginning to involve many of the ingredients of central-place foraging. I would also argue that this is important, not because it makes the hominids human but rather because it sets up a situation in which there would be clear advantages accruing to individuals with superior abilities to communicate and to play what I have called social chess. The point is not that we are seeing modern humans two million years ago, but that we are seeing non-human hominids with a behavioural configuration which gave advantage to some of the extraordinary abilities that we humans now take pride in. The next two million years saw the maturation of those abilities.

Let me return briefly to the possibility that scavenging opportunities helped to create the possibility for central-place foraging behaviour. In Fig. 7.5 there is a large parcel of nutrients, well-guarded in this instance. From the archaeological evidence, it seems clear that by two million years ago

Fig. 7.5. Lions at a zebra kill, Ngorongoro Crater, 1984. Photograph by Glynn Isaac.

hominids had begun to cut up large carcasses and to carry pieces of them to particular places. There are good reasons why they may have sought to do the cutting at the carcass, which is often a scene of quite fierce competition for access. Quite simply, carcasses are not healthy places for relatively small and unprotected hominids to be; but once they had invented the means to cut off bits of carcass, they gained an opportunity not available to other animals, that of detaching useful bits and then going away. Scientists are currently exploring a series of hypotheses connected with the behaviour of cutting and carrying. Rick Potts, for example, has suggested that our sites are actually caches of stones to which carcasses were carried for cutting up. However, I am more interested in the possibility that the hominids were cutting bits off carcasses and then taking them away to places where they could eat in safety and at leisure. The motivation was to go somewhere safe and calm, and only secondarily may such places have become sites where food changed hands and mouths socially. Of course, we have still to work out how this final transition to full-scale home-bases and collective consumption took place.

Finally, I should like to emphasize the importance of resisting the temptation to make these early hominids, *Australopithecus* and *Homo erectus*, too human. All too often in the past, we have depicted our ancestors in our own image; and yet they must have been very different. For example, if you are made of a hundred pounds of meat and live in the African savannah, it is probably very unwise to curl up at the foot of a tree when the sun sets and go to sleep. This being the case, it seems highly probable that the early hominids followed the good old primate pattern of climbing up a tree at sunset, and going to sleep. In how many other ways, we may wonder, were our ancestors closer to the typical primate than they were to that most unusual species *Homo sapiens*?

8

The origins of human intelligence

R.E. Passingham

Introduction

It is plausible that evolution could have created the human skeleton; but it is hard to credit that it created the human mind. In just a few million years, evolution came up with sapient man, a creature quite unlike anything the world had ever known. The mental gap between man and ape is immense; and yet evolution bridged that gap in a short space of time.

How could it be that the *mental* distance between a person and a chimpanzee could so outstrip the *morphological* differences between them? The problem is much like a puzzle that concerns molecular biologists. In recent years they have been looking at the genetic material in various animals, including ourselves. They have discovered that the genetic distance between a man and a chimpanzee is surprisingly small: in fact, it is smaller than the distance between a mouse and a rat (Kohne 1975). And the story is similar if comparisons are made of structural proteins: in this respect people are closer to chimpanzees than are mammals taken from related genera (King and Wilson 1975). Yet people do not look very like chimpanzees; simple measurements of the relative proportions of the body reveal very large discrepancies between man and ape, differences as large as those between animals that belong to different suborders (Cherry *et al.* 1978). In other words, the *morphological* distance between man and chimpanzee is very much greater that you would expect from the *genetic* distance between them.

This apparent discrepancy can be resolved once it is appreciated that it is possible for a small genetic change to have very far reaching effects on bodily growth and form. We believe some genes to be regulatory genes that affect the course of growth by controlling the rate of change or the timing of developmental processes. A slight alteration in such genes could alter the development of the adult form in a radical way (Gould 1977). Geneticists have looked at mutant fruit flies (*Drosophila melanogaster*). In some of them, whole body parts are transposed or altered, so that, for example, legs appear where there should be antennae or parts of the mouth. Yet it is probable that these bizarre deformations result from relatively simple changes in the gene complexes controlling development (North 1984).

Another example is provided by the giant panda (*Ailuropoda melano-leuca*). Zoologists have been puzzled by giant pandas because they look so different from bears; indeed there have even been suggestions that they might really be big racoons. The issue is now settled because molecular biologists have been able to measure the genetic distance been giant pandas and bears, and it turns out that indeed they are bears (Sarich 1976). But it has been argued that the transformation to the giant panda may have required only a change of perhaps five or six basic genetic messages (Davis 1964). The reason why the morphological distance can be much greater than the genetic distance is that simple changes in regulatory genes can have radical effects.

I want to argue that it may be possible to bridge the mental gap between man and ape in much the same way. We need appreciate only that simple changes that affect development can have revolutionary effects. I am going to suggest six such changes. Three relate to the development of the size and organization of the brain. Three concern the way in which the brain acquires information during postnatal development.

Brain

Size

The brain is the only one of our organs that is unusual in its development. Our heart, lungs, kidney, and liver are of the size we would expect for a primate of our build (Stahl 1965). But our brain is three times larger than it should be for a primate as heavy as we are (Passingham 1982).

There are two obvious ways in which the growth of an organ such as the brain could be promoted. One is to increase radically the rate at which growth takes place; the other is to maintain the same rate but to permit growth to occur over a longer period. We can tell which of these methods is used by plotting the rate at which the human brain develops and the length of time for which it grows.

The development of the human brain (from conception to the age of two years) is shown in Fig. 8.1. The black dots give the weight of the brain in individuals at different stages of development. Birth usually occurs at 40 weeks or so.

We need to compare the rate of development with that typical of other mammals. I have plotted data for a few large-brained mammals; the points show the weight to which the brain has grown by the time of birth. The values for the primates are shown as open circles, and the values for some sea-mammals as circles enclosing crosses. It is impressive that the brain of the seal (*Leptonychotes weddelli*) has grown to 400 grams in 44 weeks, and the brain of the dolphin (*Tursiops truncatus*) has reached 770 grams in 51 weeks. It will be seen that the human brain had attained much the same weights by the same

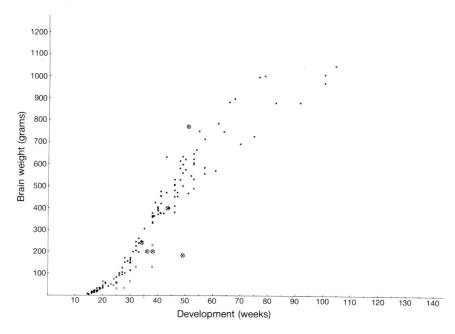

Fig. 8.1. The growth of the human brain (black dots) from conception to two years after birth. The data were kindly provided by Professor J. Dobbing. The open circles show the weight of the brain at birth in 13 non-human primates, and the large circles with crosses show the weight of the brain at birth in six sea-mammals. These values are positioned along the axis of development, according to the number of weeks before birth. The data for the animals are taken from Sacher and Staffeldt (1974). Figure taken from Passingham (1985). With permission from S. Karger AG, Basel.

times. We can form a proper judgement of how good the fit is by using these data to predict how large we would expect the brain of a mammal to be after any particular number of weeks of development. At six months after birth the human brain is roughly half its adult size. On the basis of the data from other primates, we estimate that a brain that has grown for as many weeks should weigh 679 grams (Passingham 1985). In fact it weighs 700 grams. The fit is remarkable. What it tells us is that the human brain does not attain its impressive size by growing at a uniquely fast rate. Instead it grows at much the rate we would expect for a mammal, but continues to grow for much longer. The device for producing so large a brain is a simple one. We need suppose only an alteration in genes controlling the timing of growth.

It is one thing to say that the human brain continues growing until it is three times the size expected for a primate of our build. It is quite another to say what this means in terms of intellectual capacity. We need some calibration,

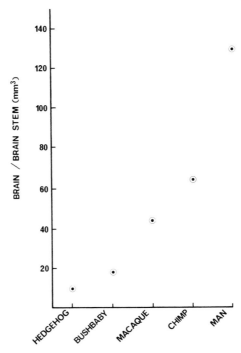

Fig. 8.2. The volume of the brain (mm³), relative to the volume of the brain stem (mm³) in man, three non-human primates (chimpanzee, macaque monkey, and bushbaby) and the hedgehog.

some way of estimating the advantage given. One way is to compare the brains of different mammals in the way shown in Fig. 8.2. This plots the volume of the brain (in relation to the volume of the brain stem) in man, three primates, and the hedgehog (*Erinaceus europaeus*). The distance between the brains of man and chimpanzee (*Pan troglodytes*) is greater than the distance between the brains of chimpanzee and hedgehog. We do not regard chimpanzees as just clever hedgehogs, and we should not regard ourselves as just clever chimpanzees. The increase in brain size may have been easy to execute, but it was revolutionary in its effects.

Proportions

In comparing the size of the brain in man and chimpanzee, we have assumed that the two brains are constructed in much the same way. But if the human brain is built more effectively, then the mental gap between man and chimpanzee might be widened further.

One way of considering the matter will be to compare the relative development of the various parts of the brain in man and other primates. It would be of particular interest to chart the development of those higher areas in the neocortex that we believe to be particularly concerned with cognitive functions. These regions are sometimes referred to as the 'association areas' of the brain, on the assumption that they are involved not in the immediate analysis of sensation or the direction of movement, but rather in understanding the relationships between events in the world.

Unfortunately, the boundaries of these areas are difficult to chart, and it has not yet proved possible to take reliable measurements of the relative size of the association areas in a series of primates including man. However, there is an indirect way of approaching the question. All the different areas of neocortex receive much of their information from a relay station called the thalamus, which lies centrally under the neocortex. The thalamus can easily be divided into its component nuclei, each nucleus being a collection of many nerve cells. Each nucleus of the thalamus sends information to particular regions of the neocortex, some to sensory areas, others to motor areas, and yet others to the association areas. The relative development of the different regions of the neocortex is reflected in the relative development of the different nuclei of the thalamus. Thus, if we measure the size of the nuclei in different species, we may gain some idea of the relative importance of the cortical areas to which they are linked.

Fig. 8.3 charts the relative development of the various nuclei of the thalamus in 39 primates, including man. It compares 18 prosimians (the lower primates), 18 monkeys, 2 apes (the chimpanzee and gorilla), and man. For each group the figure shows the size of the nuclei as a proportion of the whole thalamus.

It is immediately evident that there are radical differences between the groups in the relative development of the various nuclei. The most obvious example are the lateral nuclei. These nuclei send information to a very wide area of association cortex. The lateral nuclei form only 26 per cent of the thalamus in prosimians; in monkeys the figure is 41 per cent, and in apes 49 per cent; but in man it is as high as 71 per cent. The ape brain is not just a larger version of the monkey brain, and the human brain is not just a larger version of the ape brain. These brains differ markedly in the relative development of the component parts.

There is something else of interest in this figure. The brains are arranged in order of increasing size. The average volume of the brain is 13 600 cubic millimetres for the prosimians, 51 980 for the monkeys, and 426 231 for the apes; the value for man is 1 251 847. The differences between the groups in the proportions of the nuclei reflect differences in the size of the brains. The human brain is the largest, and it is in the human brain that the lateral nuclei form the biggest proportion of the thalamus. It is obviously not valid to

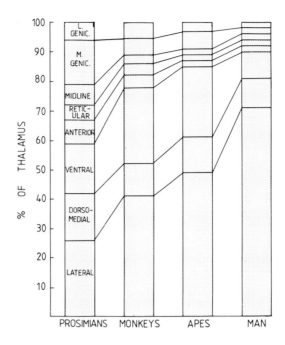

Fig. 8.3. Eight nuclei of the thalamus as labelled on the left-hand column. The proportions that these nuclei form of the total thalamus are shown in the columns: for prosimians, monkeys, apes, and man. The figure is further explained in the text. *L. genic.* = lateral geniculate; *M. genic.* = medial geniculate; *midline* = midline nuclei; *reticular* = reticular nuclei; *anterior* = anterior nuclei; *ventral* = ventral nuclei; *dorsomedial* = dorsomedial nuclei; and *lateral* = lateral nuclei. The data on the size of the nuclei were kindly supplied by Professor R. Bauchot. Figure taken from Passingham et al (1986). With permission from S. Karger AG, Basel.

assume that brains of different size are organized in exactly the same way.

Two questions arise; the first is how the alterations in proportions are brought about. It is possible that it was quite a simple matter to bring about the restructuring of the human brain. Comparisons of living species, as in Fig. 8.3, suggest that there is already a trend in primate evolution for certain areas to become more important in brains of increasing size. It appears that the trend was followed in the evolution of the human brain. If the changes in overall size and the changes in proportions are interrelated, then a relatively simple genetic change might alter both radically.

But there is a second question. What is the effect of that change on cognitive capacity? It does not matter whether the change is simple to bring about; however, if it is achieved it could vastly increase the mental gap between man and ape. If brains of different sizes also differ in the relative importance of the various specialized regions, then they should not be regarded simply as different versions of the same brain expressed at different sizes. They also differ in degree of specialization, and we should expect that difference to be evident if we compare the performance of the brains. If we were to triple the volume of the chimpanzee brain, while keeping the proportions unaltered, it would still be no match for the human brain.

Organization

Our comparison between the human and chimpånzee brain has made a further assumption. Even if two brains were to be of the same size and construction, they might differ in the efficiency with which they were organized. There is one respect in which the human brain is unique in the organization of its functions.

In all mammals the brain divides into two hemispheres. The brain is organized so that the cortex of the left hemisphere receives sensory information about the world to the animal's right, and also directs movements of the limbs on the right side. Correspondingly, the cortex of the right hemisphere looks after things on the left.

However, the arrangement is usually that the association cortex interprets information from both sides of the world and influences action with any of the limbs. As far as we can tell, the association cortex of the left hemisphere duplicates to a great extent the functions of the association cortex of the right hemisphere. Indeed, in one experiment on monkeys, one hemisphere was removed without obviously compromising the ability to solve difficult cognitive problems; the animals performed as well as monkeys with both hemispheres intact (Nakamura and Gazzaniga 1978).

This arrangement is not efficient. It would clearly be more sensible to make full use of all the tissue available. If there is a division of functions, such that some are the province of the left and some of the right hemisphere, more processing of information will be possible.

There are one or two cases in which we now know that functions have been reallocated in this way. In songbirds such as the canary (*Serinus canarius*) and chaffinch (*Fringilla coelebs*), areas within the left hemisphere are specialized for the control of the production of song (Nottebohm 1981). And in Japanese monkeys (*Macaca fuscata*), tissue in the temporal association cortex of the left hemisphere plays a predominant role in the analysis of the calls that the animal hears (Heffner and Heffner 1984).

But there is only one species in which the reorganization has been radical; and that is man. In the human brain there are differences between the functions of the association areas of the left and the right hemisphere; and this is true whether we consider the frontal, parietal, or temporal lobes. Damage to the association cortex in the left hemisphere tends to disrupt the ability to handle verbal tasks, and damage to the association cortex on the right tends to lead to disabilities on visuo-spatial tasks (Kolb and Whishaw 1985).

The capacity for language is very expensive in the amount of cortical tissue required to support it (Jerison 1976). Thus, the evolution of that capacity in our ancestors may have demanded that duplication in function be minimized. The less the duplication, the greater the amount of available space (Levy 1977).

For whatever reason that the reorganization occurred, its effects must be radical. It increases yet again the mental gap between man and chimpanzee. It is not just that we have a big brain; it is also uniquely proportioned and organized with especial efficiency.

Programming

The three factors mentioned above determine the processing capacity of the human brain. But the efficiency with which people handle information is not determined simply by the structure of the brain. It is greatly affected by the efficiency with which information is fed into the brain. In comparing the mental gap between man and chimpanzee, we have, until now, supposed that their brains are programmed with equal efficiency; but of course they are not.

Teaching

All human beings, however simple their culture, acquire information by being taught by their fellows. A chimpanzee, on the other hand, acquires its knowledge of its natural habitat by first-hand experience. It interacts with its physical and social world, and discovers what is the right thing to do. This is not to say that the chimpanzee does not learn from others. There is good evidence that a variety of birds and mammals can learn by observation of others and by imitation of their actions; but there is, as yet, no convincing evidence that in nature any animal deliberately alters its behaviour to tutor others (Passingham 1982).

For animals, we may say, it is the world that selects what is to be done. Some acts are successful and some not, and the individual learns by trying and then monitoring the outcome. Things are different when we teach. Then it is the teacher who selects which of the various possibilities is to be correct. The teacher tells the pupil what is right and what is wrong. In other words it is the teacher rather than nature that provides the feedback.

The teacher also performs another function. In nature it is the animal itself that determines the order in which it meets with particular experiences. But the teacher can choose the best order in which to expose the pupil to the material. Rather than throwing the pupil in at the deep end, the teacher sets the easy tasks before the more complex ones and thus shapes the performance of the pupil by stages.

One way of demonstrating the advantages of teaching is to take an animal that is not taught in nature, such as a chimpanzee, and then to teach it ourselves. It turns out that, in the laboratory, chimpanzees can be taught accomplishments that an untutored chimpanzee could never learn if left to its own devices. For example, it is within the capacity of a chimpanzee or gorilla, if instructed, to learn some of the elements of the sign-language, Ameslan, used by the deaf in America (for one review see Passingham 1982). It is controversial whether the apes have advanced far enough to be said to learn a language; but there is convincing evidence that apes can be taught to understand the use of names (Savage-Rumbaugh *et al.* 1980; Gardner and Gardner 1985; Savage-Rumbaugh and Rumbaugh 1985). Furthermore, they can acquire a very large repertoire of signs; one chimpanzee called Nim learnt 125 signs in 44 months (Terrace 1979).

Could the apes learn if they were merely exposed to a community of people who communicated in sign-language? In other words, would the apes progress far by imitation even if they were not formally taught? It turns out that although they may learn an occasional sign in this way, real progress is only made if a tutor intervenes. The most effective way of training the apes is to take their hands and mould them into the correct configurations (Fouts 1972). Furthermore, the tutor can encourage learning by feedback on correct usage and by giving some incentive, whether in the form of food or tickles. Finally, the ape will make little of an intricate conversation, unless it is first deliberately exposed to the simpler elements. The teacher plays a crucial role.

Education

It is not simply that people are taught whereas animals learn without guidance. It is also the case that people are taught through much of their childhood and adolescence, whether informally at home or formally at school. Our education consists of a whole series of lessons, some in one thing and some in another. Later achievements are possible because the student can draw on information and skills acquired in previous lessons.

One chimpanzee has been educated in just this way (Premack and Premack 1983). Her name is Sarah. From the age of five-and-a-half years until she was seven, she was taught to use plastic symbols. Since then, for over ten years, she has been educated three to four hours a day and for five days a week. In this time she has been set a great variety of different cognitive problems.

Of what advantage, in terms of mental achievement, is such an education? We need tests that measure intellectual capacity. One common form of IQ tests for people gives a series of items that obeys some rule, and then asks the subject to complete a new series by applying that rule. The material can be letters, or numbers, or abstract designs.

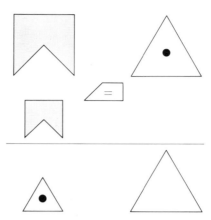

Fig. 8.4. Example of a problem given to the chimpanzee Sarah, for which she must find the solution on the basis of analogy. The problem is explained in the text. Figure taken from Gillan *et al.* (1981).

Sarah has been tested on a simple version of such a test (Gillan *et al.* 1981). An example is given in Fig. 8.4. The problem is give above the line. On the left a large shape sits over a smaller version of the same shape. On the right there is a large triangle. Sarah's task is to pick one of the two designs shown under the line, and place it under the triangle. In this case the correct solution is to pick the small triangle. Her task is to see the relation between the figures on the left and complete the series on the right by analogy.

Of course, no one would doubt that with enough practice on a single test of that sort, Sarah could learn the correct solution by rote; since for each attempt she makes she is told whether she is right or wrong. But rote learning is no indicator of intelligence. To assess her ability, it is necessary to present Sarah with totally new problems for just one trial each. If she genuinely understands the principles involved, she should be able to solve each problem at the first attempt. Sarah has been assessed in this way. She is first given practice on a large series of problems, so that she learns that she is required to reason by analogy. She is then given a test series of novel problems for one trial each. The problems differ in the shapes, colours, sizes, and markings of the designs; sometimes the principle is a change in size, sometimes in colour, and sometimes in the marking of the designs. Overall, Sarah gave the right answer on 45 out of the 50 problems.

Perhaps she was filling in the missing item by trying to make the whole look symmetrical, rather than by reasoning about the relations between items. It is possible to find out by presenting her with different material where the correct solution does not promote symmetry. An example of such an item is illustrated in Fig. 8.5. On problem A, a key opens a lock; the solution is there-

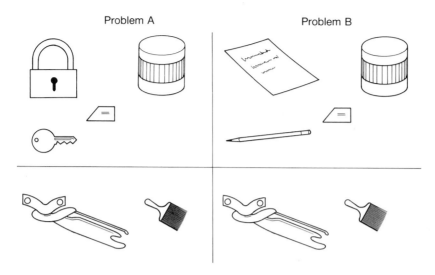

Fig. 8.5. Example of two problems given to the chimpanzee Sarah, for which she must find the solution on the basis of analogy. The problems are explained in the text. Figure taken from Gillan *et al.* (1981).

fore to pick the can-opener because that opens a paint tin. But perhaps the chimpanzee might choose a can-opener, not because she appreciated the analogy, but rather because it was the thing that she most associated in her mind with a tin. Again, it is possible to find out, by giving problem B. Here the pencil marks paper, and the solution is therefore to pick the paint-brush because it marks the tin. If Sarah gets both problems right, then she must be operating by analogy. In fact, on a test series of novel problems, Sarah was right on 15 out of 18 problems.

Sarah has not been assessed only on analogies. She has been presented with many types of problem, involving number, proportions, causality, conservation of mass, and other principles (Premack and Premack 1983). What is remarkable about her performance is that she seems to grasp abstract concepts very easily. On many problems she quite outclasses chimpanzees who have not had the advantage of her long education (Premack and Premack 1983). Her education has taught her how to think.

Teaching in language

The way that Sarah is taught is slow and cumbersome. If we wish to educate her in some new concept, we have to expose her to real cases to which that concept applies. Suppose that we teach the mathematical concepts of proportion, such as a half or a quarter. This has been done by Woodruff and

Premack (1981). The procedure was to show Sarah half a glass of liquid, and then to see whether she appreciated that it was the same as a disc that had been cut in half. With patience, it should prove possible to tutor such an animal in many concepts by showing it the various situations that exemplify the concepts.

But that is not how much of our own education proceeds. Certainly, in the nursery school, the children learn to match designs and numbers. But, as time goes on, new concepts are introduced in a totally new way, that is by *definition*. We do not need to teach the concept of an eighth or a sixteenth by exposure to real instances of those proportions. A sixteenth can be defined in language as half an eighth. The mathematical symbol '*x*' could, in principle, be taught by exposure to all the possible numbers; but it is quicker to define the symbol in language as a variable number.

If concepts and ideas are taught in words, the teacher can now teach about things that are not present or visible. Events in the past, places at a distance, complex abstract ideas, all can be described in words alone. There is no need to leave the schoolroom. If education proceeds by the accumulation of knowledge, then it is essential that information be acquired rapidly. But if the subject must view every place, and study concrete situations, then learning will be so slow that there will not be time to get to the higher reaches of thought. Einstein would still be fumbling around with elementary proportions.

That language helps to promote human thought is recognized by all. But it has been common to assume that the benefit occurs because people actually think *in* language. However, there is no conclusive evidence that we do think in words (Allport 1983). This is not to deny that sometimes we say things over in our heads when we wish to keep them in mind or to grapple with a difficult idea. The claim is only that the basic code in which thinking occurs may not be the words of language.

The most striking evidence for this view comes from patients who have language disabilities. One such patient was examined by Levine *et al.* (1982). The patient had had a stroke and was totally unable to speak at the time of the examination. Strikingly, he had also lost the ability to talk silently to himself; he heard no inner speech of any kind. Yet this did not stop him thinking. He was given the Ravens Matrices as an intelligence test. Each item of this test consists of a short series of designs; the subject has to detect the rule obeyed by the series and then supply the final design of the series. This test certainly makes demands on the ability to reason; yet the patient's score was within the top five per cent for the population. Though the patient was unable to think in the sounds of speech, he could reason intelligently.

It is important to distinguish two different ways in which language might contribute to thought (Allport 1983). The first is that we might *think* in language; and it is not certain that this is true. The second is that new information might be acquired by being *transmitted* in language; and it is quite clear that this is true. The patient could never have acquired his impressive ability to reason had he not been taught in language. Human cognitive performance depends crucially on the way in which we communicate with each other in language; we are the only animal to do so. Einstein was not only taught, and taught for many years; he was also taught in language.

Conclusion

I have argued that we can account for the vast mental gap between man and chimpanzee if we compound the effects of certain simple changes. Man has not only acquired a bigger brain, that is a larger and more efficiently organized computer; he has also adopted a new programming language. Thus, during development, information is both better acquired and better processed.

It has been traditional to suppose that the gap between man and animal occurs because man has a soul and the chimpanzee does not. The view taken in this paper is less romantic.

References

Allport, A. (1983). Language and cognition. In *Approaches to language*, (ed. R. Harris), pp. 61–94. Pergamon, Oxford.

Cherry, L.M., Case, S.M., and Wilson, A.C. (1978). Frog perspective on the morphological differences between humans and chimpanees. *Science*, **200**, 209–11.

Davis, D.D. (1964). The giant panda: a morphological study of evolutionary mechanisms. *Fieldiana Mem. (Zool.)*, **3**, 1–139.

Fouts, R.S. (1972). Use of guidance in teaching sign-language to a chimpanzee. *J. Comp. Physiol. Psychol.*, **180**, 515–22.

Gardner, H.A. and Gardner, B.T. (1985). Signs of intelligence in chimpanzees. *Phil. Trans. R. Soc. London*, **B308**, 159–76.

Gillan, D.J., Premack, D., and Woodruff, G. (1981). Reasoning in the chimpanzee: I. Analogical reasoning. *J. Exper. Psychol. Anim. Beh. Proc.*, **7**, 1–17.

Gould, S.J. (1977). *Ontogeny and phylogeny*. Harvard University Press, Cambridge, Mass.

Heffner, H.E. and Heffner, R.S. (1984). Temporal lobe lesions and perception of species-specific vocalizations by macaques. *Science*, **226**, 75–6.

Jerison, H.J. (1976). The paleoneurology of language. *Ann. N. Y. Acad. Sci.*, **280**, 370–82.

King, M.-C. and Wilson, A.C. (1975). Evolution at two levels in humans and chimpanzees. *Science*, **118**, 107–16.

Kohne, D.E. (1975). DNA evolution data and its relevance to mammalian phylogeny. In *Phylogeny of the primates*, (ed. W.P. Luckett and F.S. Szalay), pp. 249–61. Plenum, New York.

Kolb, B. and Whishaw, I.Q. (1985). *Fundamentals of human neuropsychology*. Freeman, New York.

Levine, D.N., Calvanio, R., and Popovics, A. (1982). Language in the absence of inner speech. *Neuropsychol.*, **20**, 391–409.

Levy, J. (1977). The mammalian brain and the adaptive advantage of cerebral asymmetry. *Ann. N. Y. Acad. Sci.*, **299**, 264–72.

Nakamura, R.K. and Gazzaniga, M.S. (1978). Hemispherectomy versus commissurotomy in the monkey: one hemisphere can be better than two. *Exper. Neurol.*, **59**, 202–08.

North, G. (1984). How to make a fruit fly. *Nature*, **311**, 214–16.

Nottebohm, F. (1981). Laterality, seasons and space govern the learning of a motor skill. *Trends in Neurosci.*, **4**, 104–06.

Passingham, R.E. (1982). *The human primate*. Freeman, Oxford.

Passingham (1985). Rates of brain development in mammals including man. *Brain Beh.Evol.*, **26**, 167–175.

Passingham, R.E., Heywood, C.A. and Nixon, P.D. (1986). Reorganization in the human brain as illustrated by the thalamus. *Brain Beh. Evol.*, **29**, 68–76.

Premack, D. and Premack, A.J. (1983). *The mind of an ape*. Norton, New York.

Sacher, G.A. and Staffeldt, E.F. (1974). *Amer. Nat.*, **108**, 593–615.

Sarich, V. (1976). The panda is a bear. *Nature*, **245**, 218–20.

Savage-Rumbaugh, E.S. and Rumbaugh, D.M. (1985). The capacity of chimpanzees to acquire language. *Phil. Trans. R. Soc. London*, **B308**, 177–86.

Savage-Rumbaugh, E.S., Rumbaugh, D.M., Smith, S.T., and Lawson, J. (1980). Reference: the linguistic essential. *Science*, **210**, 922–5.

Stahl, W.R.G. (1965). Organ weights in primates and other mammals. *Science*, **150**, 1039–41.

Terrace, H.S. (1979). *Nim*. Eyre Methuen, London.

Woodruff, G. and Premack, D. (1981). Primitive mathematical concepts in the chimpanzee: proportionality and numerosity. *Nature*, **293**, 568–70.

9

Darwinism and human purpose

Richard Dawkins

Darwin delivered two shocks to the vanity of our species. The first inspired the contemporary caricatures, and led to his theory being widely known as the 'monkey theory'. He showed that we are close cousins to those most caricaturable clowns of the zoo, monkeys and apes. Previous chapters in this book have dealt with the common ancestry of monkeys, apes, and humans in some detail, and readers can judge for themselves how shocking the knowledge about their species' kinship still is. But the second shock delivered by Darwin was quite different, and I suspect that it has not worked its way through our collective system quite as well as the first. Darwin not only gave us an entirely new set of unwelcome relations. He provided a new rationale for our existence; a new answer to the ultimate questions of human purpose.

Even today, if we ask what are we for, why are we here, the popular answers are still rather smug, self-important ones. Man is created in the image of God; we are here to assist in the working out of God's purpose. Other animals and plants are placed here for our use. Those who have rejected the old religions often substitute an equally smug right to exploit other living creatures for our own purposes. Even those who imagine that they have dethroned God from their minds still act as if man was created in some God's image. If it is taken to its logical conclusion, Darwin's theory leads to a rather less flattering answer to the question of the ultimate purpose of human existence. I shall explain the point in modern language, but I like to think it is how Darwin would put it if he were alive today.

The body is a machine programmed to preserve and propagate the genes that ride in it. The rationale for this is very simple. The genes that exist in the world are copies of genes that succeeded, in the past, in surviving and making copies of themselves. The vehicles of that success were ancestral bodies. Modern bodies have therefore inherited the very characteristics that made ancestral bodies successful in passing on their genes. Therefore when we look at modern bodies we can expect them to exhibit those characteristics. They will tend to behave as if they had been designed to pass on their genes. In practice they will work for their own survival, and the survival of their offspring and other close kin, for the simple reason that the offspring and kin themselves have a good chance of containing the same genes. An animal is a survival machine for the genes that built it. We too are animals, and we too are survival machines for our genes.

That is the theory. In practice it makes a lot of sense when we look at wild animals. Wild animals obviously work hard to preserve their own lives and those of their offspring. They do not indulge in self-centred hedonistic pleasures. Many of them work extremely hard to feed and protect their children, often at great cost to themselves. They don't always get it right. Sometimes they make mistakes which are fatal for themselves or their children. But it is hard enough (though not quite impossible) to find authentic examples of wild animals working assiduously and energetically for some goal which is *not* concerned with preserving and propagating their own genes.

It is very different when we look at ourselves. We appear to be a serious exception to the Darwinian law, and my task in the remainder of this chapter will be to account for it. It obviously just isn't true that most of us spend our time working energetically for the preservation and propagation of our genes. To be sure, we are mostly very concerned with our own individual survival, and if we have children we are very concerned that they should survive too. But we don't always work hard to *get* children, as naïve Darwinism should predict. Naïve Darwinism has no explanation for the widespread practice of contraception. Many of us deliberately have fewer children than we are economically capable of rearing.

Worse, from the literal-minded Darwinian point of view, many people adopt the children of others and go to great trouble and expense to rear them. In nature, any genetically inherited urge to adopt and rear unrelated offspring would rapidly disappear from the population, ruthlessly weeded out by Darwinian selection. In nature, the only way to persuade another animal to look after your child is to deceive it elaborately into thinking that it is their own. This is how cuckoos make their genetic living. Yet in some human civilizations the desire to adopt is so strong that the mother of an unwanted baby can sell it for money. If we carry the parallel to its logical conclusion, it's as if the *cuckoo* was paid, and paid by her victim! Similarly, artificial insemination would seem to the naïve Darwinian an ideally trouble-free method for a male to propagate his genes, yet in our civilization artificial insemination agencies actually pay their sperm donors!

The Darwinism that is surprised by these familiar facts about the aims and purposes of modern human beings is naïve, literal-minded Darwinism. What would non-naïve Darwinism look like, in its approach to understanding human purpose?

There is an ambiguity in the way we use the language of purpose. When we say 'the purpose of an aeroplane's tail is to stabilize the plane', we are saying something about the intention of the designer. If we look at a bird, it is evident that its tail does much the same thing. If the bird didn't have a tail it would pitch and roll like an aeroplane without a tail. It is natural, therefore, to use the same kind of language: the *purpose* of a bird's tail is to stabilize it in flight; the purpose of a hedgehog's spines is to protect it; the purpose of a rabbit's fur is to keep it warm; and so on. But as we have seen, everything about animals and plants that looks as if it had been designed for a purpose has in fact been shaped by the slow sculpting of natural selection. I shall call this kind of purposiveness 'Purpose Type 1' or 'survival value'. In a way, Purpose Type 1 is not really purpose at all, for there is no need to postulate a designer. Birds have efficient and correctly shaped tails simply because they are built by genes that have come down through generations of successful birds. By definition the *ancestors* of a modern bird were successful: unsuccessful birds left no descendants. A bird was unlikely to be an ancestor unless it had a correctly shaped tail. Therefore modern descendant birds contain the genes that happened to have the effect of building correctly shaped tails. That is why tails, and all other attributes of animals and plants, look as if they had been designed by a clever mind with a purpose in view. But the purpose is pseudopurpose—'Purpose Type 1'.

Aeroplane tails really *have* been designed by a clever mind with a purpose in view. I call this kind of purpose, Purpose Type 2. Purpose Type 2 is the kind of purpose we are familiar with from our own designs, schemes, and goals. When we say that the purpose of an aeroplane's tail is to stabilize the plane, it is Purpose Type 2 that we are talking about. We are talking about a goal in the mind of a designer.

My thesis is that Purpose Type 2 is, in fact, an evolved adaptation with a survival value (or Purpose Type 1), in the same sense as a feather, an eye, or a backbone has a survival value. Brains have evolved with various capacities that assist the survival of the genes that made them. The brain can be seen as a kind of 'on-board computer', which is used to control the body's behaviour in ways that are beneficial to the genes that built it. Among the useful capacities of the brain are the ability to perceive aspects of the outside world; to remember things; to learn the consequences of actions—which ones have good results and which ones have bad results; the ability to set up simulated models in imagination; and—here is the point of the argument—the ability to set up purposes or goals in the sense of Purpose Type 2. The capacity to have a mental goal or purpose (Type 2) is an adaptation with a survival value or purpose (Type 1), in just the same sense as the capacity to run fast, or the capacity to see clearly.

I said that the brain was an on-board computer. This doesn't mean that it works in exactly the same way as a man-made electronic computer. It certainly doesn't. But the brain does the job of an on-board computer, and some of the principles and techniques of computer science apply in brains. Now, why should it be useful for an on-board computer to set up goals, to have purposes (Type 2)? Do man-made electronic machines in fact have Purposes (Type 2)?

Yes they certainly do. This doesn't mean that they are conscious. It is still reasonable and useful to talk of a machine having a goal, even if it is not conscious. Think of a guided missile tracking a moving target like an aeroplane. The missile is controlled by its own on-board computer, which detects the position of the target by radar, by heat, or by some other equivalent of sense organs. The discrepancy between the present positions of plane and missile is measured, and the motors and steering surfaces of the missile are manipulated by the computer in such a way as to reduce the discrepancy. If the target plane takes evasive action, spiralling and twisting and turning, a good missile automatically takes countermeasures. It shows flexible, versatile behaviour to close the gap between itself and the plane. The missile behaves as if its computer contains a mental picture of its target, a Purpose Type 2.

Cannon-balls didn't have this property. They were simply lobbed by the cannon in the direction of the target. Once on their way they didn't home in on the target; they didn't track the evasive twists and turns of the target. A cannon-ball has no on-board computer, and no Purpose Type 2. It was, of course, designed with a purpose in mind—in fact much the same purpose as motivates the designer of the guided missile. In their *design* purposes, the two kinds of projectile don't differ much. Where they differ is in how they work. The cannon-ball is just a lump of iron. The guided missile has its own computer on board, and its computer contains within itself a Purpose Type 2. It behaves as if carrying a mental picture of its own goal around with it.

Now, just as human designers have found it expedient to build into their weapons an on-board computer with its own Purpose Type 2, so natural selection has built into some living organisms the same facility. Just as a guided missile is a more effective weapon than a cannon-ball, so an animal with a brain and flexible goal-seeking behaviour is a more effective predator, say, than an animal without a brain, or with a stereotyped and inflexible brain.

Some living things manage without computers at all. Plants don't move, and don't have brains. But most animals move around, and move around in sophisticated ways more reminiscent of guided missiles than of cannon-balls. Many of them are rather simple kinds of guided missiles. Maggots follow a delightfully simple rule in guiding themselves away from light. The maggot swings its head from side to side, while its computer compares the light intensity on the two sides, and instructs the muscles to move the maggot in such a way as to equalize them. Experimenters showed this by switching on a light whenever the maggot turned to the left, and switching it off every time the maggot turned to the right. This caused the maggot to circle to the right indefinitely. In nature, of course, light does not turn itself on and off in such an annoying manner, and the behavioural rule works as an effective guidance system for moving towards darkness. Let's not be snobbish about it either. There is some evidence that new-born human babies use much the same side-to-side swinging technique to find the breast.

Animals employ a range of increasingly sophisticated guidance systems paralleling the techniques developed by human engineers. Dragon-flies hunting smaller insects dive and swoop, twist and turn, with all the flexibility of a man-made guided missile. They use their large eyes to detect the position of the moving target; they use their brain to compute the necessary movements of their steering surfaces, and they frequently intercept and catch the target. A sensible way to interpret their behaviour is to say that their brain is set up as if it had a goal or purpose (Type 2). I suspect that the kinds of computation that go on inside a dragon-fly's head when it tracks a gnat are probably rather similar to the computations that go on in the missile as it tracks a fighter plane. The same is probably true of the parallel between the sonar systems in bats, whales, and human submarines.

I don't know whether dragon-flies and bats are conscious of their prey, or whether they are just wired up like automatic guided missiles, which are, after all, very effective. My suspicion is that dragon-flies are probably not conscious, but bats may be, and whales almost certainly are. I know that I myself am conscious of my goals, and I presume that other people are too. I suggest that conscious goal-seeking is the latest advance in the cybernetic technology of nature, an advance, perhaps over the dragon-fly which is about as great as the advance of the rapidly wheeling and turning dragon-fly over the maggot swinging its head alternately left and right, and blundering in vaguely the right direction.

Now, one of the main virtues of an advanced goal-seeking machine is its flexibility. It's easy to reprogram it to seek a different goal. A captured enemy missile may be programmed to seek out and destroy its original creators. The very property that makes the missile so effective in achieving its goal—its flexibility and versatility—that very property makes the machinery easy to subvert to a new purpose.

This brings me back to my original problem. Why is it that humans appear to seek goals that have nothing to do with the survival and propagation of their own genes? Why do we set up goals like making money, composing a brilliant cantata, winning a war, or an election, or a game of chess or tennis? Why aren't all our goals related to the one central goal of propagating our genes?

The answer I am giving is this. It is our *capacity to set up goals*, and to reprogram our goal-seeking machinery rapidly and flexibly, that has been built into us by natural selection. This goal-seeking capacity, and its inherent properties of flexibility and reprogrammability, is an immensely useful piece of brain technology. Useful, that is, in propagating genes. That is why it evolved in the first place. But by its very nature it carries the seeds of its own subversion. Precisely because of its flexible reprogrammability, it is highly prone to seeking new goals.

But there is a paradox in this virtue of flexible reprogrammability. If a machine is *too* ready to change its goals it will never achieve any of them.

What is required is some mixture of flexibility in setting up new goals, coupled with tenacity and inflexibility in pursuing them. Our brains are flexible enough to be reprogrammed away from goals that are directly concerned with gene survival, and adopting a new and arbitrary global purpose, perhaps one inspired by religion, by patriotism, by 'sense of duty', by 'loyalty to the Party'. But they are inflexible enough, once reprogrammed, to spend an entire lifetime seeking the new global goal. And—yet another paradox—to show great versatility and flexibility in the setting up of new *sub*-goals in the service of the inflexibly pursued main goal. This subtle interplay between flexibility and inflexibility is something that we should work hard to understand, for it has vitally important consequences.

To return to my main theme, what natural selection has built into us is the *capacity* to seek, the capacity to strive, the capacity to set up short-term goals in the service of longer-term goals, eventually the capacity for foresight. When natural selection originally built up these capacities, the shorter and longer-term goals were always in the service of the ultimate long-term goal of gene survival. But it was in the nature of flexible goal-seeking that this original ultimate goal was itself capable of being subverted. From the selfish genes' point of view, their survival machines became too clever by half. An excellent innovation in nervous-system technology, flexible reprogrammability, over-reached itself as far as its original Darwinian purpose was concerned.

From our point of view, as the flexible computers involved, our shaking off of thraldom to our original purpose of propagating the selfish genes can be seen as an exhilarating liberation, as exhilarating as Wordsworth found the French Revolution: 'Bliss was it in that dawn to be alive: but to be young was very heaven.' I suspect that our species is indeed still young in its new-found liberation. Although the human brain has been capable of great flexibility for a long time, the take-over by the on-board computers probably ran away with itself in a big way when the rise of language enabled large groups of people to set up *shared* goals, which could be pursued over more than one lifetime. *One* inventor may set himself the task of improving methods of transport, and produce the wheel. *Generations* of inventors, each building on the accumulated achievements of their predecessors who shared the same goal, are capable of producing the supersonic airliner and the space shuttle. This is a new kind of evolution, superficially similar to the old, and producing advances in technology which mirror the old genetic advances, but at a rate which may be a million times faster. The speed of this new kind of evolution, coupled with the ease with which the human brain can be reprogrammed to adopt a new major goal, and the single-minded tenacity with which it can pursue that goal once adopted, are frightening, for they could promise great danger. It's all too easy for rival groups of humans to adopt incompatible goals—for example patriotic or sectarian claims over disputed territory. Like advanced guided missiles, we are apt to pursue those goals with relentless tenacity and great flexibility in setting up efficient sub-goals, the sub-goals of war. Finally, the extreme rapidity of cultural evolution, driven by the cumulative pursuit of shared technical goals, makes possible the deployment of devastating technical weapons. We must hope that our species' 'blissful dawn' will not turn as sour as the French Revolution did for Wordsworth. There are *some* grounds for hope. That same flexibility, versatility, and foresight, which threatens us by throwing our stately Darwinian evolution into runaway overdrive, could also be our salvation.

Index

Index